THE LAST-MINUTE GUIDE TO GI SUBSPECIALTY BOARD EXAMINATION

Sam Wyntail MD

Wyntail Publications LLC

CONTENTS

Title Page

Copyright

Epigraph

Foreword

1. Esophagus   1

2. Stomach   29

3. Small Intestine   55

4. Colon   73

5. IBD   109

6. Liver   129

7. Bile duct and Pancreas   191

8. Miscellaneous   217

9. Abbreviations   251

FOREWORD

GI Board examinations have been historically an intense and intrusive experience for new and established gastroenterologists. The exam format has changed a lot in recent years which has made the examination palpably easier. The pass rate for the Boards is around 95% for first timers. So it is quite possible that you do not need any help in passing the boards nor do you need to take time off and spend hundreds of dollars in getting ready for the examination. However, the knowledge, the minutiae, the esoteric stuff and the answers to the 'Gotcha questions' needed to pass the GI boards, have not always been applicable to GI practice. We worry if the preparation and performance was adequate until we have that final congratulating message from ABIM.

Here is a knowledge bank based on guidelines, prep questions and other resources to help you with the exam preparation. This knowledge bank helped me literally *nail* the GI Boards. I am finally done with the GI Boards, never having to worry about it again. Rather than discard this resource, I want to share it with everybody so that you may also ace the Boards. During the summer of 2023, I had to take extended time off for unforeseen health issues but it also gave me time to update the study material and guidelines while recuperating.

I am publishing this book via Amazon Kindle without any professional help to keep the costs to a minimum and the final price nominal. It took me several weeks to edit, format and proofread but it may not still be perfect. I intend to keep it updated every few months. I hope you find this guide useful in preparing for the GI boards. If there are any errors or suggestions, please email me at Samslastminuteguide@gmail.com.

Best wishes!

Sam Wyntail MD

August 23, 2023

1. ESOPHAGUS

INTRODUCTION

1. Esophagus is 25 cm in length and extends between upper esophageal sphincter (UES) next to pharynx and low esophageal sphincter (LES) next to the stomach
    - Travels behind heart and trachea and through the diaphragm to end into the stomach
    - Symptoms of the esophagus such as pain from Boerhaave's syndrome (spontaneous rupture of esophagus) are often referred to the back

2. Zenker's diverticulum
    - Usually seen in 7 or 8th decade of life
    - Associated with lack of compliance of muscles in this area
    - Protrudes through the Killian's triangle
        - Between the transverse fibers of cricopharyngeus and oblique fibers of lower inferior constrictor muscle
    - Small Zenker's can be treated by cricopharyngeal myotomy
    - Be familiar with barium image of Zenker's diverticulum

3. Esophagus is lined by stratified squamous epithelium until the squamocolumnar junction or the Z line where it transitions into columnar lining of the stomach
    - Barrett's esophagus if normal squamous lining of the esophagus is replaced with intestinal epithelium

4. Irregular Z line extends < 1 cm from the GE junction
    - No biopsies recommended
    - If > 1 cm consider short segment Barrett's

5. Schatzki's ring is a circular membrane of mucosa and submucsoa without muscularis that forms at the Z line
    - May cause intermittent dysphagia
    - Often associated with hiatal hernia, sometimes with Eosinophilic esophagitis (EoE)
    - Upper surface lined by squamous epithelium, lower surface with columnar epithelium
    - Treated with dilation (Savary or balloon), needle knife, tissue biopsy

6. Inlet patch of esophagus
    - Incidental finding of an isolated patch of columnar mucosa just distal to the UES
    - Congenitial anomaly with limited clinical significance
    - Lined by heterotopic gastric epithelium

- No therapy in the absence of symptoms

7. Upper 1/3rd of the esophagus has predominant skeletal muscle, the lower 2/3rd smooth muscle
- Dermatomyositis affects only skeletal muscles and peristalsis is not affected. Presents with oropharyngeal dysphagia, proximal esophageal dysmotility
- Dermatomyositis also presents with skin rash around eyelids and hands, proximal muscle weakness with elevated CPK with + ANA and Anti-SAE antibody

8. Muscles of the esophagus
- Longitudinal muscles of the esophagus shorten esophagus
- Circular and right crura of the diaphragm contribute to LES pressure
- Nitric oxide (NO) is the neurotransmitter for relaxation of LES

9. Esophagus has 3 points of narrowing:
- UES, broncho-aortic constriction and LES
- Pill esophagitis involves esophagus near aortic arch due to decreased lumen and lowest amplitude of peristaltic waves in this area. May cause ulcerations and strictures
    - Causes of pill esophagitis include antibiotics, K+, Fe, NSAIDS, Fosamax, Quinidine, Emepronium, Crizotinib, Vit C

10. Anything that is not lodged in the esophagus or <12 mm will pass through so long as asymptomatic

11. Oropharyngeal dysphagia presents with choking and coughing, history of cerebrovascular accident (CVA) or nasopharyngeal regurgitation
- Manage with videofluoroscopy/ barium swallow evaluation
- Ptosis associated with dysphagia consistent with Occulopharyngeal muscular dystrophy which is a AD genetic condition

12. Globus pharyngeus (or globus) is the sensation of a lump in the throat and may be described as a foreign body sensation, a tightening or choking sensation
- Managed by reassurance

GERD

1. GERD is the commonest GI disorder presenting with pyrosis (heartburn) and regurgitation

2. Causes of GERD
    - Loss of LES tone
    - TLESR
    - Hiatal hernia
    - Delayed gastric emptying
    - Increased gastric volume
    - Obesity
    - Abnormal esophageal motility
    - ZE syndrome and increased acid production
    - Duodenogastric reflux

3. GERD with pressure like chest pain in the absence of red flag symptoms *r/o Cardiac causes*
    - Needs Cardiology consult

4. Red flag signs or symptoms requiring EGD
    - Weight loss
    - Dysphagia
    - Odynophagia
    - Anemia
    - Anorexia
    - GI Bleeding
    - Persistent vomiting
    - First degree family history of GI cancer

5. Endoscopy for chronic GERD symptoms and 3 or more risk factors for Barrett's
    - Caucasian male
    - Central obesity
    - Age > 50 years
    - Smoker
    - First degree relative with Barrett's or esophageal cancer

6. EGD for GERD evaluate for
    - Erosive esophagitis
    - Diaphragmatic hiatus (Hill grade of flap valve)
    - Axial hiatal hernia length
        - Barrett's esophagus

7. In chronic heartburn, commonest EGD finding is normal exam

8. LA grade for esophagitis
    - A: < 5 mm erosions
    - B: > 5 mm erosions that doesn't extend between 2 folds
    - C: Erosion/ulcerations that extends beyond 2 folds but < 75% of circumference
    - D: Ulcerations/ erosions extend > 75% of the circumference

9. In suspected GERD with negative endoscopy, *next step is reflux monitoring OFF therapy* to establish the diagnosis.
    - GERD without visible mucosal injury on EGD is non-erosive **reflux disease (NERD)**
    - Diagnosed through ambulatory pH monitoring

10. Ambulatory pH monitoring
    - Catheter type pH electrode placed 5 cm above LES
    - pH capsule placed 6 cm above Z line

11. No further testing to prove GERD when patient has
    - Barrett's esophagus
    - Grade C/D esophagitis
    - *Abnormal acid exposure time off PPI > 6% with pH <4*
        - Reflux symptom association and mean nocturnal impedance are not diagnostic for GERD but adjunctive to *acid exposure time* (most important parameter)

12. Symptom association is *most reproducible* finding in pH monitoring

13. Ambulatory reflux monitoring preferred over symptom questionnaires for definitive diagnosis of GERD
    - Response to PPI is not diagnostic of GERD
    - Endoscopic findings not diagnostic unless grade C, D esophagitis or Barrett's

14. Infrequent GERD use BRAVO instead of sleuth testing
    - pH capsule study with unproven GERD
    -While evaluating for anti-reflux surgery, use *baseline acid exposure time >* symptom association and nocturnal baseline impedance

15. Patients with atypical presentation with no red flag symptoms and not responding to PPI therapy
    - Check pH off PPI

16. Transient lower esophageal sphincter relaxation (TLESR) is a major GERD

mechanism
- Unrelated to gastric acid production
- Not associated with swallow
- Lasts 10-45 seconds (normal is < 10 seconds)
- Medullary GABA(B) neuron stimulation stops the TLESR

17. Reduced TLESR
- Baclofen (GABA receptor agonist)
- Lean body mass
- Gastric outflow obstruction

18. Increased TLESR
- Obesity
- Obstructive sleep apnea
- Increased colonic fermentation
- Sleep disturbance

19. Upright reflux
- Shorter duration
- Usually associated with TLESR
- Postprandial
- Not during sleep
- Poor response to surgery and PPI therapy

20. GERD at night associated with
- Prolonged acid exposure
- Reduced LES
- Poor esophageal clearance
- Hiatal hernia
- Severe esophagitis

21. In patients with Reynaud's syndrome and GERD symptoms check for Antinuclear antibody (ANA) to rule out Systemic Sclerosis

22. Laryngopharyngeal reflux (LPR)
- Positive predictive value of Laryngoscopy is low. Poor agreement on LPR findings
- EGD findings not helpful in LPR
- Impedance > Laryngoscopy or empiric PPI therapy for diagnosis of LPR (ACG 2020)
- Impedance testing off meds in LPR is to document NO GERD.
- Ruling out GERD rules out LPR
    - Positive GERD during Impedance test does NOT *rule in* LPR
- Treated with BID PPI x 3 months.

23. EGD should not be used as the method to establish a diagnosis of GERD-related asthma, chronic cough, or LPR.
- No diagnosis of LPR based on laryngoscopy findings alone and additional testing should be considered
- Response of extraesophageal symptom to PPI therapy is not confirmatory of GERD
- Lifestyle modifications, sphincter augmentation, alginates, cognitive behavioral therapy and neuromodulators may help with extra esophageal symptoms

24. Extraesophageal manifestation of GERD
- Sinusitis
- Dental erosions
- Otitis
- Laryngitis
- Asthma
- Chronic cough, aspiration
- Pulmonary fibrosis

25. Patient with normal acid exposure but high symptom correlation has Reflux hypersensitivity
- Functional chest pain, treat with tricyclics

26. Step-up therapy for GERD
- Lifestyle
- Sucralfate
- H2 receptor antagonists (H2RA)
- PPI

27. Lifestyle management of GERD (ACG 2021)
- Weight loss in obese patients
- Avoiding meals within 2–3 hr. of bedtime.
- Avoidance of tobacco products/smoking
- Avoidance of "trigger foods"
- Elevating the head of bed for night time

28. PPIs over H2RA for erosive esophagitis
- PPI 30–60 min before a meal rather than at bedtime
- Discontinue PPI in patients with GERD with NO erosive esophagitis or Barrett's esophagus, and whose symptoms have resolved with PPI therapy
- Use the lowest working PPI dose
- No routine addition of medical therapies in PPI non-responders
- Maintenance PPI therapy indefinitely or antireflux surgery for patients with LA grade C or D esophagitis
- On-demand/or intermittent PPI therapy for heartburn symptom control

in patients with non-erosive reflux disease (NERD)

29. Adjunctive pharmacotherapy for GERD phenotype (AGA 2022)
    - Alginate antacids for breakthrough symptoms
    - Nighttime H2 receptor antagonists for nocturnal symptoms
    - Baclofen for regurgitation or belch predominant symptoms
        - No Baclofen in the absence of objective evidence of GERD
    - Prokinetics for coexistent gastroparesis
        - No prokinetics for GERD unless gastroparesis
    - No sucralfate for GERD except during pregnancy

30. First line agents to treat GERD in pregnancy are antacids containing Al or Mg

31. Acid pocket is a layer of unbuffered content that sits within the proximal stomach in the area of cardia and fundus. Buffering by alginates may reduce post prandial reflux

32. Heartburn, regurgitation, and non-cardiac chest pain without alarm symptoms is treated with a 4-8 week trial of single-dose PPI therapy.
    - With inadequate response, increase to twice a day or switch to a more effective agent once a day
    - Patients with non-cardiac chest pain need EGD and/or reflux monitoring for GERD
    - No barium swallow needed to diagnose GERD
    - GERD unresponsive to PPI- *Ask patient how they take PPI*
    - Rabeprazole has the highest potency amongst PPI therapy. Pantoprazole the least

33. Refractory GERD
    - First step is optimization of PPI therapy
    - If obese, recommend weight loss
    - If young patient with aspiration episode and nonresponsive to high dose PPI, EGD and motility to r/o achalasia
    - Esophageal pH monitoring performed OFF PPIs if the diagnosis of GERD has not been established by
    - Esophageal impedance-pH monitoring performed ON PPIs for patients with an established diagnosis of GERD
        - Previous pH study
        - EGD showing long-segment Barrett's esophagus or LA grade C or D esophagitis.

34. Grade C or D (and select B) esophagitis, repeat EGD in 2 months to confirm healing

35. GERD symptoms and noncardiac chest pain on high dose PPI and negative EGD needs impedance testing

36. High resolution manometry (HRM) may help in evaluation of treatment nonresponsive noncardiac chest pain

37. Impedance testing while ON medication
    - Previous positive pH study
    - Large hiatal hernia
    - Esophagitis or Barrett's seen at EGD

38. In suspected GERD with extraesophageal manifestations, *evaluate first for non-GERD causes*
    - Currently, there is no single diagnostic tool that can conclusively identify GERD as the cause of extra esophageal symptoms
    - Without typical GERD symptoms (Isolated extraesophageal symptoms), reflux testing before PPI therapy
    - If both extraesophageal and typical GERD symptoms, a trial of twice-daily PPI therapy for 8–12 wk. before additional testing
        - If 12 week PPI therapy of extraesophageal symptoms doesn't help then objective testing for pathologic GERD

39. If PPI therapy is continued in unproven GERD beyond 12 months, offer endoscopy with wireless reflux monitoring off PPI therapy to justify appropriateness of therapy

40. Deprescribing PPI (AGA Feb 2022)
    - All patients on PPI should have a regular review by primary care for ongoing indications for use
    - Twice-daily PPI dosing should be considered for once daily PPI
    - Discontinuing long-term PPI may cause transient symptoms due to rebound acid hypersecretion.
    - Either dose tapering or abrupt discontinuation is acceptable
    - Discontinue PPIs based solely on the lack of an indication and not because of concern for adverse events

41. Patients who should not be considered for PPI discontinuation:
    - Complicated GERD
        - Severe erosive esophagitis
        - Esophageal ulcer
        - Peptic stricture
    - Barrett's esophagus
    - Eosinophilic esophagitis
    - Idiopathic pulmonary fibrosis
    - High risk for upper gastrointestinal bleeding

42. In chronic GERD, Magnetic sphincter augmentation (MSA - LINX procedure) > PPI BID

43. Bariatric surgery with GERD, prefer Roux-en-Y gastric bypass (RYGB)
    - Criteria for Obesity surgery for GERD is BMI> 30

44. Sleeve gastroplasty associated with sleeve stenosis in ~ 5%
    - Presents with GERD and obstructive symptoms
    - Treated by balloon dilation at incisura; if not responsive then Roux-en-Y gastric bypass

45. GERD on PPI
    - With large hiatal hernia greater than 3 cm consider laparoscopic fundoplication
    - With no hiatal hernia consider laparoscopic fundoplication or magnetic sphincter augmentation

46. Prior to invasive anti-reflux procedures we need (AGA 2022)
    - Confirmatory evidence of pathologic GERD
    - Exclusion of achalasia
    - Assessment of esophageal peristaltic function
    - Lack of response to PPI may predict lack of response to surgery

47. In Regurgitation as primary PPI-refractory symptom and abnormal GERD by objective testing, consider antireflux surgery or Transoral incisionless fundoplication (TIF)
    - TIF done only if hiatal hernia is < 2 cm and who do not have LA grade C or D reflux
    - Antireflux surgery for patients with objective evidence of GERD
        - Severe reflux esophagitis (LA grade C or D)
        - Large hiatal hernias
        - Persistent, troublesome GERD symptoms

48. Consider MSA as an alternative to laparoscopic fundoplication for patients with regurgitation who fail medical management.
    - *Roux-en-Y gastric bypass* to treat GERD in obese patients who are candidates for bariatric surgery

Barrett's Esophagus

1. Barrett's is replacement of the normal stratified squamous lining of the esophagus by goblet cell containing intestinal epithelium
   - Diagnosis of Barrett's only with intestinal metaplasia (not with gastric metaplasia)

2. Exams should use Prague classification (C and M criteria) to describe Barrett's
   - C is circumferential length of Barrett's and M is maximum length of Barrett's

3. 10% of chronic GERD have Barrett's esophagus (BE), 50% of Barrett's have no GERD symptoms

4. Columnar mucosa should be at least 1 cm of length minimum for diagnosis of Barrett's esophagus
   - No biopsy of normal or irregular Z line < 1 cm without lesions

5. Barrett's esophagus has tongue of salmon colored mucosa
   - If no tongue of abnormal mucosa then Intestinal metaplasia of gastroesophageal (GE)junction
   - Minimum of 8 endoscopic biopsies in possible Barrett's and Seattle protocol for longer segments

6. Screening for Barrett's - One time screening only
   - Chronic GERD symptoms and 3 or more risk factors
     - Caucasian male
     - Central obesity
     - Age > 50 years
     - Smoker
     - First degree relative with Barrett's or esophageal cancer
   - No survival benefits with screening or surveillance

7. Screening for Barrett's by both white light and chromoendoscopy
   - Endomicroscopy may be used as adjunctive techniques to identify dysplasia.
   - Swallowable nonendoscopic capsule device combined with biomarker is an acceptable alternative for screening
   - Screening may be cost effective for Barrett's with dysplasia

8. WATS-3D and Seattle protocol biopsy sampling compares well with white-light endoscopy with Seattle protocol biopsy sampling
   - ACG guideline update April 2022 does not make a recommendation for

or against it or p53 stain or TissueCypher

9. Barrett's with indefinite dysplasia, optimize therapy and repeat EGD in 3-6 months

10. Barrett's with low grade dysplasia (LGD)
    - Confirm with an expert pathologist and repeat EGD with biopsies in 6 months
        - If still LGD then repeat EGD in 1 year
    - PPI once per day in the absence of esophagitis
    - ACG guideline update April 2022 suggests eradication therapy

11. Barrett's with high grade dysplasia (HGD)
    - Biopsies q 1 cm all 4 quadrants
    - Endoscopic mucosal resection (EMR) of any nodularity
    - Rate of progression to cancer is 6% per year

12. Progression in Barrett's risk score
    - Male sex- 9 points, Cigarettes 5 points, Barrett's 1 point per cm, Confirmed low grade dysplasia- 11 points
    - < 10 points, annual risk ~ 0.1%
    - 11-20 points, annual risk~ 0.7%
    - > 20 points, annual risk ~ 2.1%

13. Management of Barrett's
    - At least once a day PPI recommended for Barrett's
    - Nissen's fundoplication not recommended as an antineoplastic measure
    - Surveillance
        - Long segment BE (≥3 cm) at 3-year intervals
        - Short segment BE (<3 cm) at 5-year intervals
    - Smoking cessation
    - *Endoscopic mucosal resection (EMR or ESD) of all visible lesion*
    - Endoscopic ablation of all visible BE

14. No surveillance when a patient is no longer a candidate for Endoscopic eradication therapy (EET)

15. Optimal age of last surveillance in Barrett's without dysplasia
    - No comorbidities stop at 81 years
    - Mild comorbidities is 80 years
    - Moderate comorbidity is 77 years
    - Severe comorbidities is 73 years

16. Patients with Barrett's esophagus on BID dose of porton pump inhibitors (PPI) and ongoing symptoms

- Test pH while ON medications to evaluate for possible fundoplication

17. Barrett's esophagus unresponsive to RFA, optimize acid suppression with PPI
    - Cryotherapy can be considered

18. Barrett's recurrence after RFA is most common at GE junction

19. Once complete eradication of intestinal metaplasia (CEIM) accomplished via EET EGD surveillance for Barrett's(ACG March 2022)
    - LGD 1 y and 3 years after CEIM and q2 years thereafter
    - HGD and IMC at 3 months and 6 months and then annually after EET

20. Surveillance biopsies after endoscopic ablation is independent of the length of the original BE segment

21. After CEIM, random biopsies should be taken of (AGA July 2022)
    - Esophagogastric junction
    - Gastric cardia
    - Distal 2 cm of the neosquamous epithelium
    - All visible lesions

22. *Any esophageal cancer (or rectal cancers) greater than T2 or N0 needs neoadjuvant therapy*
    - T1 esophageal lesions managed by EMR
    - No bronchoscopies for esophageal cancers below carina

23. Elderly patient with EG junction outlet obstruction with weight loss needs EUS or alternative imaging to rule out a mass lesion

24. Esophageal squamous dysplasia or early squamous cell cancer of esophagus, well differentiated, non-ulcerated, without submucosal invasion > 15 mm, manage with ESD
    - < 15 mm EMR or ESD
    - Surgery not recommended

25. Squamous cell ca of the esophagus
    - Associated with sub-saharan Africa, east and central Asia
    - Tobacco and alcohol use
    - Consumption of high temperature food and beverages
    - Nutritional deficiencies
    - Dietary nitrosamines

26. Increased risk of SCC of esophagus in
    - Tylosis (leukoplakia, esophageal papilloma and hyperkeratosis)

- Lye ingestion
- Plummer vinson syndrome (Fe deficiency with esophageal web)
- Fanconi's anemia (bone marrow failure syndrome)
- Achalasia
- Scleroderma

27. Early T1, nodular Barrett's with dysplasia, well differentiated without ulceration > 20 mm ESD over EMR
    - < 20 mm, then ESD or EMR

28. Obesity, white race, tobacco use and male sex associated adenocarcinoma in Barrett's

29. Roux-en-y gastric bypass associated with decreased progression of Barrett's

Motility

1. Esophageal high resolution manometry (HRM) is widely adopted in clinical practice and helps evaluate esophageal motility
   - Distal latency (DL) >4.5 seconds
   - Integrated relaxation pressure (IRP) <15 mm Hg
   - Distal contractile integral 450-8000 mm Hg

2. If distal latency (DL) is low ie. <4.5s in 20% of swallows with normal Integrated relaxation pressure (IRP) then patient has distal esophageal spasm (DES)
   - No need to have normal contractions
   - Treat with peppermint oil which is a smooth muscle relaxant
   - If on opioids, stop opioids
   - Myotomy if lifestyle and medical management have not been helpful

3. If DCI> 8000 mm of Hg(> 20%) with normal IRP and DL then Jackhammer esophagus (Hypercontractile esophagus)
   - Increased cholinergic drive to the esophageal smooth muscles
   - Treatment is PPI therapy, calcium channel blockers (diltiazem 60 mg 3 x daily), POEM

4. If 70% of contractions with DCI>100 but <450 or 50% DCI<100 then *ineffective esophageal motility*
   - If 50-70% ineffective contractility inconclusive then barium swallow of bolus or lack of contraction reserve on multiple rapid swallows
   - Associated with GERD, Barrett's, Diabetes mellitus (DM) with neuropathy, alcoholic neuropathy and collagen vascular diseases
   - Treated by optimization of acid suppression therapy
      - Chewing well
      - Maintaining an upright posture x 2-3 hours after meals

5. If IRP is > 15 mm of Hg, then consider achalasia or esophagogastric junction outlet obstruction (EGJOO)

6. **Achalasia**- Incomplete EGJ relaxation
   - Increased IRP
   - Normal IRP rules out achalasia

7. There are 3 types of Achalasia
   - *Achalasia type 1* (Classic)- Swallowing shows no changes in panesophageal pressure.
   - *Achalasia type 2*- Low amplitude panesophageal pressurization

- *Achalasia type 3*- High amplitude panesophageal pressurization.

8. *Achalasia type 1* (Classic)- Swallowing shows no changes in panesophageal pressure.
   - No pressurization of esophagus
   - Treatment by Pneumatic dilation, laparoscopic Heller's myotomy or Peroral endoscopic myotomy (POEM)
   - Routine gastrografin not needed after pneumatic dilation
   - POEM has a higher risk of GERD

9. *Achalasia type 2*- Low amplitude panesophageal pressurization
   - Isobaric panesophageal pressurization in 20%
   - Responds best to treatment
   - Pneumatic dilation (PD), laparoscopic Heller's myotomy and POEM are equivalent for therapy

10. *Achalasia type 3*- High amplitude panesophageal pressurization.
    - Spontaneous and repetitive pressurization, premature contractions in 20% (Spastic- DL< 4.5 s)
    - Treatment is POEM

11. Patient with EGJOO
    - Manometry in both supine and upright position
    - If elevated in supine position then repeat study in sitting position
    - Median IRP is elevated in supine and upright position, 20% of swallow show intrabolus pressurization and peristalsis is present
    - Evidence of some peristalsis and intrabolus pressurization on HRM
    - Manometric evidence of EGJOO is always considered clinically inconclusive
    - May cause dysphagia and non-cardiac chest pain
    - Caused by atypical achalasia, subtle cancer, Nissen's fundoplication, EoE, opioids, peptic strictures, large hiatal hernia
    - If associated with a large paraesophageal hernia, then repair paraesophageal hernia

12. HRM better than conventional line tracing for diagnosis of achalasia
    - Provocative maneuvers for obstructive symptom

13. Botox in achalasia only if patient not a candidate for definitive therapy
    - Does not alter future myotomy
    - Myotomy with fundoplication is better than Myotomy without fundoplication
       - Dor/Toupet's fundoplication
    - Serial pneumatic dilation is the most effective non-surgical treatment
    - In young patients Pneumatic Dilation of 3.5 or 4 cm/Heller's/ POEM are

more effective than 3 cm Pneumatic Dilation

14. No role for cancer screening in Achalasia though risk of squamous cell cancer is increased
   - Increased risk of esophageal cancer persists even after treatment of achalasia

15. Lap band may cause secondary achalasia

16. Consider pseudoachalasia and consider CT/ endoscopic ultrasound (EUS) if
   - Type 2 achalasia
   - Age > 55 years
   - Short duration of symptoms < 12 m
   - Profound weight loss > 20 lbs. Difficulty in passing through GE junction

17. Opioids can cause esophageal dysmotility
   - Achalasia (not type 1)
   - EGJ outlet obstruction (EGJOO)
   - Hypercontractile esophageal abnormalities
   - If patient has chronic opioid use with dysphagia and distal esophageal spasm pattern, stop opioids

18. If HRM and IRP (ie. tests for achalasia) are inconclusive for achalasia/ EGJOO with dysphagia, then consider timed barium esophagram (TBE) combined with a 13-mm barium tablet and/or endoluminal functional lumen imaging planimetry (FLIP)

19. TBE if symptoms recur after definitive therapy of achalasia
   - Pneumatic Dilation if symptoms recur after Heller's or POEM. Heller's and POEM can also be used for recurrent symptoms
   - POEM for primary failure of Heller's myotomy
   - Resistant symptoms with megaesophagus, treat with esophagectomy

20. FLIP can be used if endoscopic placement of manometry catheter fails
   - FLIP can be used to measure EGJ distensibility and cross-sectional area during invasive treatment of achalasia
   - Can be used to assess distensibility in fibrostenotic remodeling in EoE

21. HRM can diagnose hiatal hernia

22. Functional dysphagia shows NO structural abnormalities, mucosal abnormalities, GERD, EOE or dysmotility
   - Low dose antidepressant vs behavioral therapy

23. Non-peristalsis is seen in achalasia, scleroderma and amyloidosis. Dermatomyositis affects only skeletal muscles and peristalsis is not affected

24. Patients with GERD not responding to therapy may be evaluated for achalasia

25. No endoscopic surveillance needed for achalasia

26. Peristaltic reserve assessed by multiple rapid swallow sequence
    - Intact peristaltic reserve is associated with reduced dysphagia after fundoplication

27. Chaga's disease mimics achalasia
    - Chagas disease caused by Trypanosoma cruzi
    - Can also cause chronic intestinal pseudo obstruction and valvular heart disease

Eosinophilic esophagitis (EoE)

1. Disease caused by eosinophilic inflammatory response confined to the esophagus
    - Eosinophilic infiltrate is >or= to 15 per HPF

2. EoE - r/o other causes of eosinophilia
    - Vasculitis
    - Eosinophilic gastroenteritis
    - Crohn's disease
    - Connective tissue disorders
    - GERD
    - Infections
    - Drug reactions
    - Celiac disease

3. Findings:
    - Concentric rings
    - Linear furrows
    - Whitish exudates
    - Diffusely narrowed esophagus (remodeling)
    - Endoscopic image with EoE, check for atopy
        - Slide with eosinophils is EOE

4. Severity of EoE is measured by Index of severity for EoE (I-SEE)
    - The I-SEE has three domains
        - Symptoms and complications
        - Inflammatory features
        - Fibrostenotic.
    - I-SEE is used in both adult and pediatric patients with EoE.

5. Most common trigger for EoE is milk
    - Treated with Budesonide 1-2 mg twice daily after breakfast and before bedtime
    - Candida of the esophagus most common side effect of topical budesonide

6. Take biopsies from all over the esophagus at the same time as food impaction in one specimen jar

7. Six- food elimination diet includes avoidance of
    - Dairy
    - Wheat
    - Eggs

- Soy
- Seafood
- Nuts

8. In symptomatic EoE, PPI recommended over no treatment (AGA 2020)
   - Topical glucocorticosteroids over no treatment
   - Elemental diet over no treatment.
   - Empiric, 6-food elimination diet over no treatment.
   - In patients with EoE in remission after short-term use of topical glucocorticosteroids, continue of topical glucocorticosteroids over discontinuation of treatment.
      - Commonest side effect of topical budesonide is candida of esophagus
   - In patients with dysphagia endoscopic dilation over no dilation.
   - NO anti-IgE therapy for EoE

9. Dupilumab, a IL-4R alpha antagonist, is the only FDA approved therapy for EoE

10. Suspected EoE with symptoms despite low eosinophil counts.
check tryptase stains for mast cells

11. PPIs inhibit TH2 cytokine stimulated secretion of Eotaxin-3 in EoE

12. EoE can be managed by empiric food elimination diet
   - Symptom correlation, skin test, allergy based testing are not effective

13. EoE with GERD with more eosinophils in distal esophagus responds to PPI therapy
   - Post procedural pain is common after dilation in EoE

14. Esophageal Lichen planus
   - Mimics EoE with small caliber esophagus, concentric rings,
   - Middle aged women with skin, nail and mucosal involvement
   - Mainly proximal esophagus involved
   - Dense subepithelial lymphocytic infiltrate, intraepithelial lymphocytes
   - Civatte bodies - degenerating basal cells caused by autoimmune T cell mediated damage
   - Multiple eosinophilic necrotic keratinocytes
   - Treatment is by local steroids, local steroid injection and topical tacrolimus
   - Can be managed by careful endoscopic dilation

15. Eosinophilic gastritis
   - Difficult to diagnose without specifically requesting eosinophil counts

in gastric biopsies
- Criteria is > 30 eosinophils/ high power field in the stomach

16. Lymphocytic esophagitis
   - Rare < 0.1%
   - Biopsies show intraepithelial lymphocytes and no eosinophils or granulocytes

Varices and GI bleed

1. Variceal bleed is a GI emergency and major cause of death in cirrhotics
   - Clinically significant bleed indicates transfusion requirement of > 2 units per 24 hours, systolic < 100 mg hg, orthostasis > 20 mm of Hg or pulse > 100
   - Variceal rebleed occurs within 5 days of initial bleed

2. Management of bleeding varices
   - Management involves hemostasis, avoid complications and manage underlying conditions
   - Hemodynamic stabilization
   - Restrictive transfusion (Only if < 7 mg/dl)
   - Antibiotics
   - Vasoactive agent such as octreotide
   - EGD within 12 hours
   - Esophageal band ligation of varices
   - Rescue TIPS if continued bleed

3. Early TIPS following band ligation of variceal bleed in
   - Childs Pugh class C cirrhotics
   - Childs Pugh class B with active bleed at the time of band ligation

4. Factors associated with early rebleeding
   - Age > 60y
   - Renal failure
   - Ascites
   - ETOH liver disease
   - Thrombocytopenia
   - Encephalopathy
   - Intial severe hemorrhage
   - Gastric variceal bleed

5. Upper endoscopy should be performed after fluid resuscitation and within 12 hours of admission to hospital

6. Variceal bleeds are treated with broad spectrum antibiotics (third generation cefalosporins) such as ceftriaxone or cefotaxime

7. Varices are seen when pressure gradient between portal and hepatic veins is > 12 mm of Hg
   - Pressure gradient is the difference between wedge hepatic venous pressure and free hepatic venous pressure
   - Measured by hepatic vein catheterization which is invasive

or noninvasive assessments such as platelet count and transient elastography

8. Risk of variceal bleed in patients with cirrhosis
    - Location
        - Varices at GEJ have the weak support and most likely to bleed
        - Gastric fundic varices are likely to bleed
    - Size of varices
    - Appearance
        - Red wale marks
        - Cherry red spots
        - Hematocystic spots (blood blisters)
    - Clinical features of patient such as severity of liver disease, previous variceal bleed
    - Variceal pressure > 15 mm of Hg

9. Gastric varices classified as
    - Gastroesophageal varices are varices in continuity with the esophagus
        - GOV1 along lesser curvature
        - GOV 2 along greater curvature
    - Isolated gastric varices in fundus (IGV1)

10. Gastric varices with highest risk of bleeding are isolated fundic varices
    - Rectal varices treated by glue, TIPS or banding

11. Incidental isolated fundic varices in a chronic pancreatitis patient
    - Observation
    - GI bleed with history of pancreatitis and gastric fundic varices, check CT for splenic vein clot
    - If bleeding, then splenectomy

12. Cyanoacrylate for gastric varices is not FDA approved

13. Bleeding fundic varices needs emergent TIPS

14. Management of ectopic bleeding varices is TIPS with or without embolization, Balloon occluded retrograde transvenous obliteration (BRTO), if unsuccessful then surgery

15. If drugs not tolerated for primary prophylaxis of (non-bleeding) esophageal varices, consider band ligation of varices

16. Primary prophylaxis of ESOPHAGEAL varices in medium to large varices only (not in grade 1 varices)

- If no large varices, then check in 1 year and then q 3 years or with change in functional status

17. If EGD for variceal screening is negative in patient with inactive disease, recheck q 3 years

18. EGD variceal screening recheck q 2 years in compensated cirrhosis with ongoing liver injury
- EGD for variceal screening not indicated in patients with platelets > 150k and transient elastography < 20

19. If EGD shows no varices after variceal bleed, repeat in 3-6 months and then q 6-12 months.

20. If esophageal varices after banding rebleeds and patient is hemodynamically stable then repeat EGD and banding
- If rebleeds and unstable then Blakemore tube and Transjugular intrahepatic portosystemic shunt (TIPS)
- No beta blockers in active variceal bleed acutely

21. Patient with non-bleeding esophageal varices on beta blockers, repeat EGD only with decompensation

22. Mallory-Weiss tear (MWT)
- Heals in 24-48 hours
- Treatment by clipping/ banding or thermal ablation

23. Non-variceal GI bleed, EGD within 24 hours rather than within 6 hours

24. Primary prophylaxis of choice for variceal hemorrhage during *pregnancy* is *Propranolol*
- Carvedilol lacks safety data during pregnancy

25. Endoscopies for varices during pregnancy safer in second trimester

Miscellaneous Esophagus

1. Lye ingestion causes squamous cell cancer
   - Bronchoscopy only for tumors above the carina

2. Epidermolysis Bullosa Dystrophica
   - Autosomal recessive
   - Starts at birth
   - Bullous scarring skin lesion
   - Dysphagia
   - Image of leg or feet with scarring lesion

3. EGD with dilation - no antibiotics required

4. Caustic ingestion EGD early (12-24 post injury)
   - Only exception is young kid with minimal or no symptoms with alkali exploratory ingestion
   - Stricture dilation has 30-40% recurrence rate
   - In children usually accidental
   - Acid damages the stomach while alkali damages the esophagus
   - If upper respiratory symptoms then thorough evaluation of breathing apparatus

5. Esophageal biopsy of serpiginous ulcer with multiple pink inclusion bodies with nuclear moulding has Herpes simplex virus (HSV) infection

6. Image of Green stain with hyphae (GMS) in esophagus is candida of esophagus

7. A 12 mm stricture in the esophagus dilated by 12 mm/ 36 Fr Malony's
   - Size in French = 3 x size in mm

8. Downhill (upper esophageal) varices is due to blockage of superior vena cava (SVC) caused by chest tumors, retrosternal goiter and mediastinal fibrosis
   - Management is observation since they rarely bleed
   - Diagnosis is through chest CT

9. Rumination syndrome is a behavioral disorder
   - Food regurgitated and rechewed, or spit out usually few minutes after eating
   - No nausea
   - Associated with stress
   - Associated with bulimia, in adolescent females
   - Can mimic GERD

- Young person with refractory GERD with large number of post prandial proximal reflux, nonacid reflux, increased intragastric pressure and regurgitation of recently ingested food has Rumination syndrome
- Diagnosed by high resolution impedance manometry (HRIM) with postprandial monitoring
- On esophageal manometry, rumination waves (R waves) can be seen
- Diaphragmatic breathing therapy helps

10. Patient with excessive belching regardless of eating status (including fasting) with multiple instances of high impedance from proximal to distal esophagus followed by a reflux episode and negative symptoms association probability has Supragastric belching
- Diagnosed by pH impedance (ACG 2020)

2. STOMACH

GI Bleed

1. Gastric epithelium has
   - Chief cells that secrete pepsinogen
   - Enterochromaffin cells produce histamin
   - Parietal cells produce acid
   - Foveolar cells produce mucus

2. Gastrin, histamine and acetylcholine increase acid production.
   - Stomatostatin reduces acid production

3. Patients presenting to the ED with UGIB who are very low risk ie. Glasgow-Blatchford score = 0–1, can be discharged with outpatient follow-up rather than admitted to hospital
   - Glasgow-Blatchford score based on
     - Hb
     - BUN
     - SBP
     - HR
     - Melena, syncope, liver disease, cardiac disease

4. Glasgow-Blatchford score doesn't take age of the patient into account

5. Rockall risk score for GI bleed assesses mortality. Criteria includes
   - Age
   - Comorbidities
   - Presence of shock
   - Underlying diagnosis/ cause of bleed
   - Stigmata of GI bleed

6. Age and comorbidities account for most mortality in UGI bleeds

7. Peptic ulcer disease (PUD) bleed is highest in people age> 65 (60 per some sources), history of prior GI bleed and anticoagulation
   - Urgent EGD detects high risk lesions in 30-50%

8. Stress ulcers associated with
   - Coagulopathy
   - Mechanical ventilation

9. Mechanical ventilation for more than 48 hours needs PPI prophylaxis due to high risk of GI bleed

10. NSAID injury
  - NSAIDS inhibit prostaglandin synthesis by inhibiting COX
  - Injury occurs within 1-2 hours of intake
  - Starts as subepithelial hemorrhage
  - 2-4 days erosions
  - 20-25% have ulcers, 70-75% have endoscopic abnormality
  - Different people have different levels of cyto-adaptation determining ongoing damage from NSAIDS
  - Erosive gastritis in a long-distance runner, consider NSAIDS as a possible cause

11. Risk of GI bleed is highest with Naproxen and lowest with Ibuprofen both of which are non-selective NSAIDS
  - Diclofenac and meloxicam are relatively selective COX-2 inhibitors and have lower GI risks
    - GI side effects of NSAIDS are related to COX 1 inhibition
  - There are 2 COX isoforms COX 1 and COX 2
  - COX1 is present in most tissue including GI tract, kidneys and platelets
  - COX 2 is induced by bacterial products and cytokines and found in areas of inflammation

12. Misoprostol FDA approved for NSAIDS induced gastric ulcer but causes diarrhea.

13. Smokers are more likely to have PUD

14. A normal bilious aspirate can be seen in 20% of UGI bleed
  - NG lavage is not needed for UGI bleed prior to endoscopy

15. GI bleed with hematochezia and hemodynamically unstable then consider UGI bleed and an EGD

16. GI bleed with hematochezia and hemodynamically stable i.e. no orthostasis with normal BP is **lower GI bleed**

17. Patients with hematochezia and syncope with multiple bloody stools with precipitous drop in Hb have UGI bleeding.
  - Same scenario with small drop in Hb has diverticular bleed which can also cause vagal syncope

18. Acid hypersecretion can occur with systemic mastocytosis due to excessive histamine production
  - Basophilic leukemia can also cause acid hypersecretion

19. Reversal agents if INR> 2.5

20. GI bleed from an ulcer with slowly trending down of Hb is likely equilibration and doesn't need further work up

21. Pregnant woman for UGIB needs EGD with propofol

22. Patient with GI bleed on anticoagulation
   - First step is large bore IV line and resuscitation

23. Threshold for transfusion at a hemoglobin of 7 g/dL
   - Treshold is 8 mg/dl for ortho/ cardiovascular surgery and patient with cardiovascular history

24. Endoscopy within 24 hours of presentation
   - Resuscitate patient first to a Hb> 7 g/dl prior to EGD

25. Infusion of erythromycin before endoscopy for better visualization and reducing the need for second EGD and shortens the duration of stay

26. Modalities for endoscopic hemostatic therapy
   - Bipolar electrocoagulation
   - Heater probe
   - Injection of absolute ethanol
   - Clips
   - APC
   - Soft monopolar electrocoagulation
   - Epinephrine injection should not be used alone
   - Endoscopic hemostatic therapy with hemostatic powder spray TC-325 for patients with actively bleeding ulcers

27. TC-325 hemostatic powder spray may be an effective therapy for non-variceal gi UGI bleed but lesions must be actively bleeding to be effective

28. Recurrent bleeding ulcer resistant to endoscopic therapy
   - Over the scope clips
   - Hemostatic powder followed by arterial embolization since the powder lasts no longer than 24 hours

29. Ulcers > 1-2 cm are at a higher risk of rebleeding with or without therapy

30. 72 hours required for a high-risk lesion to morph into low risk lesions

31. Ulcer base and risk of rebleeding
   - Clean based ulcer 3-5% (Forrest III)

- Discharge home on PO PPI
- Pigment (flat) spot 7-10%
    - No Endotherapy and no IV PPI (*Only PO PPI*)
- Adherent clot 20-30%
    - BID PPI therapy and no endoscopic intervention
- Visible vessel 40%
    - IV PPI treatment (Rx) and Endotherapy
    - Combination of epinephrine + thermal device
    - High dose PPI for clot formation and stability
- Spurting 70%

32. Forrest classification of ulcer
    - Ia active spurting
    - Ib active oozing
    - IIa non bleeding visible vessel
    - IIb nonbleeding adherent clot
    - IIc Hematin spot
    - III clean based ulcer

33. If patient taking aspirin for primary prophylaxis without high risk of cardiovascular complications and has GI bleed
    - Stop the aspirin

34. Restart aspirin in CAD patient after GI bleed before discharge
    - Resume antiplatelet therapy in 3-7 days in high cardiovascular risk patients

35. Recurrent ulcer
    - Recheck for H pylori if H pylori was not treated recently
    - Blood causes false negative H pylori in the stomach
        - If no blood, then low probability of false negative
    - UGI bleed with an ulcer, check for H pylori

36. Clean based ulcer with dual antiplatelet therapy (DAPT)
    - Continue PPI for the duration of DAPT

37. Patient with melenic GI bleed after recent negative work up of melena needs repeat EGD

38. PPI's undergo metabolism by cytochrome p450 system via isozymes CYP2C19 and CYP3A4
    - 20% of white patients are ultrarapid metabolizers leading to a substantial decrease in PPI efficacy

39. Twice daily divided dose of PPI better than double dosing before any one meal

40. Stopping PPI suddenly leads to rebound hypergastrinemia

41. PPI therapy
    - PPI reduces rebleeding after endoscopic therapy but does NOT reduce deaths
    - NO difference between oral and IV dose of PPI
        - IV dose acts faster
    - NO difference between IV continuous drip and intermittent dose of PPI
    - PPI reduces bleeding after nonsteroidal anti-inflammatory drugs (NSAIDS)
        - Patients on NSAIDS with risk of bleeding, start PPI therapy
    - H2RA reduces symptoms with NSAIDS but does NOT reduce complications
    - Pre-Endoscopic PPI might not reduce future mortality or bleed

42. IV PPI therapy of UGI bleed downgrades ulcer bleeding stigmata and reduces the need for endoscopic intervention

43. Patients with GI bleed with comorbidities and no obvious cause should be on PPI or H2RA for a long time

44. Idiopathic bleeding ulcers (no NSAIDS or H pylori) have a high recurrence and need treatment with once daily *PPI indefinitely*

45. After succcessful endoscopic hemostatic therapy of a bleeding ulcer, use high-dose PPI therapy given continuously or intermittently for 3 days followed by twice-daily PPI therapy until 2 weeks
    - Patients with recurrent bleeding after endoscopic therapy for a bleeding ulcer need repeat endoscopy (rather than surgery or embolization)
    - Patients with bleeding ulcers who have failed endoscopic therapy need arterial embolization

46. Prophylaxis against bleed in patients on aspirin and NSAID by PPI therapy
    - Once daily PPI therapy
    - Cox-2 inhibitors increase cardiovascular risk

47. Routine monitoring of PPI side effects are not recommend in case of long term PPI therapy

48. Tetany, seizures, SVT with chronic PPI therapy may have magnesium deficiency

49. PPI with normal B12 levels but increased methyl malonic acid (MMA) and homocysteine
   - Elevated MMA and homocysteine are found with tissue B12 deficiency even with normal serum B12
   - Increased homocysteine causes osteoporosis
   - Chronic PPI may cause low grade B12 deficiency due to lack of acid to cleave B12 from foods
   - Vitamin B12 stores in the body lasts for years

50. No Grade A/ level 1 evidence for side effects of PPI other than possible enteric infections
   - Doubles the risk of C diff
   - Increased risk of COVID 19

51. OTC PPI can cause cramps and muscle weakness in some individuals

52. H2RA associated with tachyphylaxis and loss of effect

53. Long term PPI use has been associated with Fe, B12, mg and insoluble calcium deficiency
   - PPI causes B12 deficiency due to decreased cleavage of cobalamin from dietary protein

54. Potential interaction between PPI and clopidogrel has not been demonstrated in multiple trials
   - Invitro reactions of clopidogrel with Lansoprazole and Omeprazole
   - Pantoprazole and Rabeprazole not shown to interact

55. H2RA acts quickly compared to PPI's
   - H2RA does not reduce risk of bleed

56. Gastric antral vascular ectasia (GAVE)
   - Two forms of GAVE
      - 1 is splotchy, associated with cirrhosis and portal hypertension, men more than women
      - 2 is classic watermelon stomach associated with autoimmune conditions, more in women than men
   - GAVE is a slow bleed and should not cause orthostasis or hemodynamically significant bleed
   - Portal hypertensive gastropathy can coexist with GAVE
   - Treated with argon plasma coagulation (APC)

57. GAVE associated with fibrin thrombi, fibromuscular hyperplasia of lamina propria, dilated mucosal capillaries

- Superficial lamina propria hemorrhage seen in erosive gastritis
- Congestive vasculopathy in portal hypertensive gastropathy

58. Conditions associated with GAVE
   - Cirrhosis
   - CREST, Raynaud's, Sjogren's, Polymyalgia rheumatica
   - Chronic kidney disease, DM, CAD
   - Parkinson's, AML, MGUS, Hx of bone marrow tx

59. Inappropriate Hypergastrinemia indicates loss of feedback loop leading to increased acid secretion along with elevated Gastrin levels (both acid and gastrin levels are elevated)
   - Zollinger Ellison syndrome (ZE syndrome)/ Gastrinoma
   - Gastric outlet obstruction (GOO)
   - Retained antrum syndrome
   - Antral H pylori infection related to involvement of D cells that normally suppress acid by somatostatin release

60. ZE syndrome
   - Due to gastrinoma
   - ZE syndrome doesn't cause gastric ulcers. It is mainly duodenal or jejunal
   - Most accurate test is gastric acid analysis after careful withdrawal of antisecretory therapy
   - Basal acid output > 15 mEq/h in presence of hypergastrinemia is pathognomonic of ZES
   - PET dotatate is only 70% sensitive and cannot r/o ZES

61. Appropriate Hypergastrinemia (High gastrin and low Acid)
   - Fundectomy
   - Atrophic gastritis
   - Antisecretory therapy
   - H pylori pangastritis

62. Idiopathic gastric hypersecretion has normal gastrin levels

63. Dieulafoy's lesion
   - Thick-walled artery near the mucosa without overlying ulceration.
   - Common cause of unexplained acute or recurrent bleeding.
   - The large majority occur in proximity to the GE junction, the lesser curve, uncommonly in the small bowel and colon
   - Bleeding is arterial
   - No vascular abnormalities such as atherosclerosis, aneurysms or

vasculitis
- Recurrent bleed is common
- Inject with epinephrine and use thermal ablation.
- Tattoo the area for future identification
- Treatment with banding is anecdotal and may cause perforation in proximal stomach

64. Patient with multiple clinically significant GI bleed with orthostasis and repeated negative endoscopy likely has Gastric Dieulafoy's lesion

65. Cameron erosions
- Gastric side of hiatal hernia
- Mechanical erosions
- Treat with PPI or repair hiatal hernia
- Cameron erosions are more common when hiatal hernia > 5 cm

66. PEG placement in patient on DAPT is a high risk bleeding procedure
- Do not stop aspirin but stop Plavix

67. Patient with GOO, ulcers and increased gastrin levels
- GOO with increased gastric distension causes increased gastrin
- Aggressive treatment of ulcer or GOO with PPI and endoscopy and then recheck fasting gastrin levels

68. Roux-en-Y bypass can cause
- Mn deficiency presents with seizures and infertility
- Thiamine Deficiency with mental status and memory problem
- Wernicke's encephalopathy with a triad of Ataxia, ophthalmoplegia and confusion

69. Billroth 2 with Fe deficiency anemia is due to malabsorption of dietary iron and may still respond to PO iron supplementation

70. Patient with long standing gastric bypass with high INR, replace Vit K SQ or IV

71. Roux-en-Y gastric bypass associated with B1, B12, folate, fat soluble vitamins, calcium and Fe deficiency
- Sudden weight gain after RYGB may indicate gastrogastric fistula and is treated by high dose PPI therapy

72. Marginal ulcer after Roux en Y bypass associated with
- Long gastric pouch due to relative ischemia

- Smoking- most important
- NSAIDS
- DM
- H pylori infection

73. Marginal ulcers after Roux en Y bypass are reduced by short gastric pouch and PPI therapy

74. Marginal ulcers are on the jejunal side of GJ anastomosis

75. Portal hypertensive gastropathy bleeding can be managed by Beta-blockers
   - If fails then TIPS

H pylori and other Infections

1. Dyspepsia
    - *Patients > 60 years need EGD*
    - *Test and treat strategy for H pylori for dyspepsia age < 60*
    - Hierarchy of therapy for functional dyspepsia
        - PPI / H pylori therapy if positive >Prokinetic therapy >Tricyclics> Psychological counseling
    - No EGD even for alarm symptoms age < 60 (ACG 2017)
    - If gastroparesis suspected in functional dyspepsia only then motility

2. While undergoing EGD for dyspepsia, routine biopsies of gastric body, incisura and antrum for HP infection if the H pylori status is unknown. (AGA 2015)
    - *The AGA suggests following the 5-biopsy Sydney System, with all specimens placed in the same jar.*

3. During EGD for dyspepsia no routine biopsies of the duodenum to detect celiac disease. (AGA 2015)
    - In immunocompromised patients YES to obtaining routine biopsies of the normal-appearing duodenum

4. H pylori in North America
    - Antrum inflammation with increased gastrin and increased acid due to decreased somatostatin from D cells
    - H pylori in rest of the world with corpus inflammation
        - Loss of parietal cells, loss of acid, secondary hypergastrinemia and gastric cancer

5. In limited gastric intestinal metaplasia (GIM), stomach biopsy to rule out H pylori
    - Test for H pylori and eradication over no testing (Test and treat)
    - No routine use of endoscopic surveillance

6. Patients with GIM specifically at higher risk of gastric cancer include those with:
    - Incomplete vs complete GIM
    - Extensive vs limited GIM
    - Family history of gastric cancer
    - Patients at overall increased risk for gastric cancer include
        - Racial/ethnic minorities
        - Immigrants from high incidence regions
    - Needs gastric topographic mapping

- Surveillance q3 years

7. Linitis plastica not associated with H pylori

8. *AGA recommendations treating H pylori and confirm eradication in the context of GIM*

9. CagA in H pylori infection associated with
    - Duodenal ulcer
    - Cancer of the stomach
    - IceA associated with PUD
    - VacA with inflammatory response

10. Previous H pylori therapy and now with PUD with negative H pylori test, consider NSAIDS use (surreptitious possible)

11. Inappropriate hypergastrinemia (increased gastrin levels and increased acid) associated with antral H pylori infection

12. UGI bleed with an ulcer- check for H pylori

13. MALTOMA- Eradicate H pylori and biopsy in 4 weeks
    - Gastric mucosa associated lymphoma are associated with 11:18 translocation

14. Relative risk of H pylori in causing gastric cancer is highest in young patients
    - 50% of cancer H pylori related in third world
    - Most cancers associated H pylori develop in distal stomach

15. Patient with NSAIDS erosive gastritis on PPI, check for H pylori off PPI therapy and treat if positive
    - Continue PPI until H pylori eradication is confirmed

16. All patients who test + for H pylori need to be treated except pregnant women (only acid suppression)
    - Treatment offered to H pylori infected patient with gastric ca and lymphoma
    - First degree relates of patients with gastric ca
    - Serological test is the most cost effective
        - Does not distinguish between recent and old infection

17. H pylori infection associated with

- Granulomatous gastritis
- Gastric hyperplastic polyp
- Multifocal atrophic gastritis
- Lymphocytic gastritis

18. H Pylori causes non-cardia gastric cancer
    - Correa cascade of gastric cancer with H pylori
        - Normal mucosa to chronic non-atrophic gastritis to chronic atrophic gastritis to GIM to dysplasia and cancer

19. H pylori infection may have inverse association (not protective) against esophageal adenocarcinoma, autism, asthma and food allergies

20. Urease breath test if most sensitive test for H pylori. Stool antigen test is a close second with > 95% sensitivity

21. H pylori infection
    - 40% Metronidazole (Flagyl) resistant
    - 12 % clarithromycin resistant
    - Increasing resistance to fluorquinolones reported
    - In a patient with recurrent ulcers and negative H pylori, surreptitious NSAIDS use likely

22. Treatment of H pylori indicated in
    - ITP
    - History of PUD
    - Urticaria/ DM1 (Low quality evidence)
    - Asymptomatic patients at risk of gastric cancer in high risk area
    - Unexplained Fe deficiency
    - First degree relatives with gastric cancer
    - Atrophic gastritis
    - Marginal B cell Lymphoma (MALTOMA)
    - After gastric cancer resection
    - Aspirin or NSAIDS use
    - Long term aspirin users who have GI bleed
    - Functional dyspepsia

23. Patient with H pylori and possible penicillin allergy
    - Send to allergy clinic for allergy testing
    - If any test is positive for H pylori , treat it

24 Penicillin allergy- bismuth based quad therapy for H pylori

25. Rifabutin based triple therapy is for 10 days rather than standard 2 weeks

(14 days) for other regimen

26. H pylori with clarithromycin regimen with recurrence
    - Metronidazole is not as effective
    - Quadruple therapy recommended

27. H pylori recheck only after 4 weeks of completing therapy and 1-2 weeks of stopping PPI
    - Urea breath test
    - Stool Ag
    - Biopsy

28. H pylori with previous exposure to clarithromycin treat with LOAD therapy
    - Levofloxacin
    - Omeprazole
    - Nitazoxanide
    - Doxycycline

29. Vonoprazan is a potassium channel inhibitor that can be used in treatment of H pylori instead of PPI
    - Vonoprazan is better than PPI for grade C and D esophagitis and is not affected by CYP2C19 polymorphisms

30. Active GI bleed, H pylori negative, recheck H pylori as it may be false negative

31. H pylori recurrence with Duodenal ulcer previously treated with clarithromycin based regimen
    - Never retreat with clarithromycin-based regime
    - Amoxicillin and Metronidazole based combo is not effective
    - PPI + Rifabutin + amoxicillin x 14 days

32. HSV infection shows multinucleation, margination and molding

33. Dense plasma cell infiltration and mononuclear vasculitis are associated with syphilis. Diagnosed by Warthin-Starry silver stain

34. Marked lymphoplasmacytic inflammation and neutrophils associated with chronic active gastritis associated with H pylori

35. CMV associated with cytomegaly and owl's eye intranuclear inclusions

Gastric Neoplasms

1. Increased risk of gastric cancer in Peutz Jeghers syndrome and Lynch
    - Gastric cancer risk noted in MSH2
    - Check for H pylori
    - Start EGD at age 40 and q3-5 years subsequent
    - Risk of gastric cancer lower in FAP but could be higher than general population

2. Gastric adenocarcinoma and proximal polyposis of the stomach (GAPPS)
    - APC gene mutation
    - > 100 polyps in the proximal stomach with antral sparing
    - fundic gland polyps mainly but also hyperplastic and adenomatous polyps
    - High risk of gastric cancer
    - No polyposis in the colon

3. Hyperplastic gastric polyps are from inflammatory proliferation of mucous producing foveolar cells due to chronic bile exposure

4. Gastric intraepithelial neoplasia and gastric cancer
    - Treating H pylori reduces the risk by 33%
    - Colonic type of metaplasia causes cancer > 3 x small intestinal type metaplasia
    - Sudden onset of multiple seborrheic keratosis on the trunk (sign of Leser-Trelat)
    - May be associated with Acanthosis nigricans

5. Highest risk of gastric cancer in extensive and incomplete GIM

6. Endoscopic resection of early gastric cancer
    - < 3 cm (ulcerated)
    - 2 cm (poorly differentiated) lesions
    - No lymphovascular or perineural invasion
    - sm1 (No invasion more than 0.5 mm in the submucosa)

7. EMR for early gastric cancer lesions < 2 cm *differentiated only*
    - ESD for other lesions
    - Lower complications than surgery but *higher disease recurrence and LN metastases*

8. Hereditary diffuse gastric cancer
    - Autosomal dominant
    - Associated with breast cancer

- *CDH1 mutation*
- CTNNA1 mutation can also be associated
- Diffuse type signet ring cancer
- Gastrectomy between 20-30 years

9. Fundic gland polyp is related to PPI use
  - Increased risk of dysplasia in fundic gland polyp associated with FAP (not Lynch), antral gastritis and increasing size of the largest fundic gland polyp

10. Gastric cancer with normal CT scan
  - EUS to further stage for preop treatment
  - *EMR contraindicated in lesion > 2 cm or poorly differentiated*

11. Well or moderately differentiated early gastric cancer, non ulcerated intestinal type < 20 mm ESD or EMR
  - 20-30 mm ESD
  - < 30 mm well or moderately differentiated early gastric cancer, non-ulcerated, intestinal type, surgery not recommended
  - Poorly differentiated early gastric cancer any size needs surgery

12. Chromogranin a elevated in patients on PPI or H2RA

13. Carcinoid syndrome associated most often with tumors of the small bowel (midgut)

14. Suspected gastric carcinoid, first step check serum gastrin level
  - Octreotide reduces the symptoms and the growth of carcinoid metastases
  - ZE syndrome, if not identified on multiple studies, surgical exploration

15. Gastric carcinoids
  - Type 1 carcinoid is associated with atrophic gastritis and B12 deficiency with increased MCV. Increased gastrin levels. Malignancy risk < 5%
  - Type 2 carcinoids associated with Multiple endocrine neoplasia (MEN) 1
    - ZE syndrome, *check for calcium* since 25% are a part of MEN1 syndrome and have hyperparathyroidism
    - Malignancy risk ~ 10%
  - Type 3 solitary and potentially malignant and most dangerous
    - Malignancy risk is 50%
  - Histopathology slide of blue cords of cells
  - Stains for chromogranin A and synaptophysin
  - Most of carcinoids arise from small bowel

16. In multiple gastric carcinoids with increased gastrin, check stomach biopsy for atrophic gastritis

17. EMR or ESD for Type 1 gastric NET
    - EMR or ESD of Type 2 gNET
    - ESD over EMR of type 3 gNET without lymphadenopathy who do not have surgery
    - Rectal NET < 1 cm EMR or ESD

18. Patient with diarrhea and stomach ulcers unresponsive to once daily PPI but responding to BID PPI with increased gastrin, check for ZE syndrome by secretin test

19. Barium x-ray with thick gastric folds has gastrinoma
    - ZE syndrome

20. Menetrier's disease
    - Males older than 50 years
    - Protein losing enteropathy and Hypoalbuminemia
    - Hypochlorhydria
    - Increased risk of gastric cancer
    - Childhood variety may be associated with H pylori and Cytomegalovirus (CMV)
        - May resolve spontaneously
    - Adult presenting with dyspepsia, pedal edema, low albumin and giant gastric folds
    - Biopsy shows foveolar hyperplasia with large cystic dilations
    - Menetrier's disease is caused by increased signaling of epidermal growth factor receptor (EGFR) pathway

21. Causes of thickened gastric folds
    - PUD
    - ZE syndrome
    - Hypoproteinemia
    - Lymphoma/ pseudolymphoma
    - Eosinophilic gastroenteritis
    - Menetrier's
    - Tuberculosis (TB), Syphilis
    - Inflammatory bowel disease (IBD)

22. Gastric granulomas
    - Crohn's disease- commonest cause
    - Whipple's
    - Sarcoid

- Vasculitis

23. Gastrointestinal stromal tumor (GIST) lesion is from 4th layer
    - Leiomyoma is from 2 or 4 layer
    - Lipoma from 3rd layer and has no malignant potential
    - Duplication cyst- 3rd submucosal layer

24. GIST tumor on EUS
    - GIST arises from interstitial cells of Cajal
    - Spindle cells seen on biopsy
    - cKIT mutations CD117/CD 34
    - Mainly in the stomach (60-70%)
    - Tumors < 2 cm are low risk, lesions > 5 cm are high risk of malignancy
        - Resection of gastric GIST >2 cm and all nongastric GIST
    - Mitotic rate also indicates progressive disease
    - Imatinib therapy for metastatic, unresectable or recurrent disease
    - If GIST doesn't respond to imatinib, consider sunitinib

25. All non gastric GISTs and gastric GIST> 2 cm needs resection
    - Gastric GIST < 2 cm insufficient evidence for surveillance vs resection

26. Atrophic gastritis (AGA 2021)
    - Loss of gastric glands with or without metaplasia
    - Mainly due to H pylori or autoimmunity
        - Check for H pylori infection and treat if necessary
        - Check for antiparietal cell Ab and anti-intrinsic factor Ab
    - Needs to be confirmed by biopsy
    - Presence of intestinal metaplasia on gastric histology almost invariably
    implies atrophic gastritis.

27. Typical endoscopic features of atrophic gastritis
    - Pale mucosa
    - Increased visibility of vasculature
    - Loss of gastric folds
    - Light blue crests and white opaque fields
    - Biopsies from body/ antrum and incisura and any other abnormality

28. Atrophic gastritis needs surveillance every 3 years. Optimal surveillance
of autoimmune gastritis is unclear
    - Evaluate for Fe and B12 deficiencies
    - Other autoimmune disorders including thyroid diseases need to be
    evaluated

29. Patients with pernicious anemia (late-stage manifestation of atrophic

gastritis) need to have endoscopy to confirm atrophic gastritis and rule out tumors such as neuroendocrine tumor (NET)

30. Pernicious anemia and atrophic gastritis increases the risk of
    - Noncardia gastric cancer
    - Gastric carcinoid
    - Esophageal squamous cell cancer
    - Small intestinal cancer
    - Multiple myeloma

31. Causes of B12 deficiency includes
    - Autoimmune gastritis
    - PPI use
    - Pancreatic exocrine insufficiency
    - SIBO
    - Terminal ileum resection

32. Increased gastrin level in pernicious anemia

33. Autoimmune gastritis can occur as a part of polyglandular autoimmune syndrome
    - Most sensitive test for autoimmune gastritis is antiparietal cell antibody-80%
    - Anti-instrinsic factor antibody is only 50% sensitive

34. EUS preferred to endoscopy or cross-sectional imaging for the diagnosis of non lipomatous subepithelial lesions (ACG Jan 2023)
    - EUS with tissue acquisition preferred
    - No bite-on-bite biopsies in the evaluation of subspithelial lesion (SEL) before EUS.

35. FNB or FNA with rapid on-site evaluation (ROSE) sampling preferred to FNA
    - Unroofing technique when EUS-FNA or FNB is nondiagnostic
    - Symptomatic SEL (bleeding, ulceration etc.) needs resection regardless of size or a preresection diagnosis except a large GIST for neoadjuvant imatinib

36. Submucosal tunneling endoscopic resection (STER) or surgical resection for the management of SEL originating from the muscularis propria layer of the esophagus and gastroesophageal junction

37. EMR or ESD for the resection of type 1 gastric NET
    - ESD over EMR for low-grade, small type 3 gNETs without

lymphadenopathy that do not undergo surgical resection.
- EMR or ESD for the resection of <1 cm, low-grade rectal NETs

38. SEL which have an endoscopic appearance consistent with a lipoma or pancreatic rest and normal mucosal biopsies do not need further evaluation or surveillance (AGA 2022)

Functional GI Issues

1. Vagus nerve stimulation
   - Receptive relaxation
   - Acetylcholine mediated
      - Increase in acid secretion through muscarinic receptors on parietal cells
      - Enterochromaffin like (ECL) cells to release histamine
      - D cells to reduce suppressory somatostatin
   - Releases Gastrin releasing peptide (GRP) that in turn increases gastrin release from G cells

2. Replacing a PEG tube may cause diarrhea with refeeding if the tract goes accidentally through the colon

3. Chronic smoker with generalized gut pseudo obstruction has paraneoplastic syndrome from lung cancer

4. Myopathy is from dermatomyositis, systemic sclerosis, mitochondrial disease, SLE, Ehlers Danlos

5. Parasympathetic nerves excitatory to gut while sympathetic nerves are inhibitory

6. Young patient with nausea 1-2 per week on empty stomach has functional dyspepsia
   - Buspirone beneficial at 10 mg TID dose
   - Vomiting 1-2 days per week is functional dyspepsia and not cannabis hyperemesis syndrome (CHS) or cyclic vomiting syndrome (CVS) which is usually unrelenting

7. Cyclic vomiting syndrome (CVS) occurs less than once a week and is unrelenting
   - CVS often have history of migraines
   - Females
   - 3 or more episodes per year and at least a week apart
   - Minimal symptoms in between
   - Treat with Nortriptyline every night
   - Long periods of normality between episodes compared to CHS

8. Cannabis hyperemesis syndrome (CHS) occurs almost daily is unrelenting.
   - No symptom free interval
   - Gastroparesis associated vomiting WITH meals
   - Bulimia associated vomiting occurs AFTER a meal

- Cannabis needs to stopped for at least 6 month

9. Family history of migraines with severe abdominal pain few times a year that is unresponsive to treatment is likely Abdominal migraines
    - In contrast *epigastric pain syndrome occurs at least once a week*

10. Patients with poorly controlled DM and gastroparesis need good control of blood sugar to improve gastric emptying
    - 10% food remaining after 240 min (4 hours)

11. Thin young woman seeing a psychiatrist with a gastric mass, r/o trichobezoar

12. Ghrelin (hunger hormone) reduces satiety

13. Highly selective vagotomy doesn't need pyloroplasty. Non-selective vagotomy needs pyloroplasty

14. MMC occur at 3 cycles per minute
    - Solids must be < 2 cm to exit the stomach during MMC
    - Round objects > 2.5 cm and Long thin objects > 6 cm will not pass the stomach.

15. Gastric emptying
    - Liquids > solids, Digestible > indigestible, Males> females
    - Liquids empty linearly first and then exponentially
    - Solids empty via lag/ slow emptying initially and then linear
    - Migratory motor complex (MMC) empties the indigestible solids

16. Gastric emptying for solids at 100 min is normal
    - MMC 3 hours after eating is normal in small bowel16. Gastroparesis (GP) is the second most common sensory motor disorder of the stomach.
    - Commonest cause of GP is idiopathic but DM accounts for ⅓ of the the cases
    - Abdominal pain is a cardinal symptom of gastroparesis
    - Accelerating gastric emptying doesn't improve global symptoms of gastric emptying

17. Dicyclomine may reduce gastric emptying and needs to be stopped prior to gastric emptying study
    - Selective serotonin reuptake inhibitors (SSRI) and propranolol do not reduce gastric emptying

18. Scintigraphic Gastric Emptying is the standard test for the evaluation of

GP
- No Radiopaque markers (ROM) testing for diagnosis
- WMC (wireless motility capsule) testing may be an alternative
- Stable isotope (13C-spirulina) breath test is a reliable test for GP
- On gastric scintigraphy GP is defined as < 90% emptied at 4 hours
- Gold standard for diagnosing gastroparesis is solid phase gastric scintigraphy < 4 hours

19. Therapy of idiopathic/ diabetic GP
- Metoclopramide FDA approval for no more than 12 weeks
    - Risk of tardive dyskinesia is < 0.1%
- Domperidone where approved
- Both PO and IV erythromycin helpful
- 5-HT4 agonists
- Antiemetic agents for improved symptom control
- Gastric electric stimulation (GES) may be considered
- Acupuncture alone or acupuncture combined with prokinetic drugs
- Small particle diet to increase likelihood of symptom relief
- Idiopathic gastroparesis (GP) managed by low fiber, low fat
- Pyloromyotomy for GP with symptoms refractory to medical therapy
- EndoFLIP evaluation useful in checking pyloric function and predicting outcomes after peroral pyloromyotomy

20. Post infectious gastroparesis resolves with time
- Low fat low fiber diet recommended

21. Symptoms in Diabetic GP correlate poorly with emptying rates
- Symptoms related to delayed emptying, blood sugar levels and ketones
- Optimal glucose control is suggested (ACG 2022)

22. EGD with dyspepsia
- Biopsy of normal Z line or esophagus not indicated
- Biopsy of duodenum in Graft versus host disease (GVHD) for infection in immunocompromised
- Biopsy of gastric body and antrum in patients whose H pylori status is not known. Treat H pylori with improvement in dyspepsia in 20%

23. Roux-en-Y bypass with dumping syndrome, avoid food with simple sugars
- Early dumping syndrome within 1 hour of eating and caused by osmotic effect, fluid shifts and peptide hormones (VIP and serotonin)
- Fatigue, weakness, desire to lie down, tachycardia, hypotension, dizziness, cramping and diarrhea
- Late dumping occurs after 2 hours and cause by hypoglycemia due to

insulin release

24. Dumping syndrome managed by
    - Less fluids during eating
    - Rx by small frequent meals rich in complex carbs

25. Nausea and vomiting of pregnancy
    - *Treat first with B6 and doxylamine*
    - *Promethazine is second line therapy*
    - Zofran is NOT first line for nausea
    - Meals rich in proteins decrease nausea
    - Meals rich in carbohydrates worsen nausea

26. Excitatory neurotransmitter within neuroendocrine cells is serotonin or 5HT
    - Excitatory neurotransmitters for enteric nervous system is acetylcholine

27. Only low dose (NOT high dose) Octreotide induces intestinal MMC

28. Wireless motility capsule
    - Gastric emptying time < 5 hours. The pH decreases after swallowing only to increase in duodenum
    - pH drops again after the capsule enters the cecum
    - Whole gut transit time is < 73 hours
    - Colonic transit time < 59 hour

29. Buspirone is a 5-HT agonist that helps with functional dyspepsia
    - Helps with postprandial fullness, bloating and early satiety
    - Fundic relaxation and accommodation

30. Non ulcer dyspepsia, check for H pylori and teat if positive, also start a trial of PPI. If no response then start tricyclics

31. In pyloric dysfunction, G-POEM effective in case series but no randomized trials
    - Botox injection to pylorus not useful for gastroparesis

32. Hyperglycemia delays gastric emptying

33. Rapid gastric emptying can cause nausea, dyspepsia and early satiety- Dicyclomine may be helpful

34. GLP-1 agonists delays gastric emptying

3. SMALL INTESTINE

Celiac Disease

1. Celiac disease (sprue) affects proximal small bowel more than distal
   - Villous atrophy
   - Intraepithelial lymphocytes
   - Inflammation of lamina propria

2. Celiac disease has females > males

3. IgA TTG is better than IGG TTG. False negative in IgA deficient patient with celiac disease
   - Highest positive predictive value (PPV) for celiac disease is antiendomysial antibody

4. IgG antiDGP (deamidated gliadin peptide) is not a great test. Patient with anti-gliadin +ve but anti-TTG-ve probably not celiac

5. Check TTG-IgA in diagnosis of celiac disease in children < 2 years who are not IgA deficient

6. In IgA deficiency, check TTG-IgG and DGP-IgG (Deamidated gliadin peptide) to diagnose celiac disease

7. HLA DQ2/8 testing if patient with celiac disease is on a strict gluten free diet. Haplotype negative for HLA DQ 2/8 rules out celiac disease
   - Positive test doesn't automatically rule in celiac disease

8. One year for celiac panel to normalize on a gluten free diet

9. EGD with biopsies needed for confirmation of celiac disease
   - TTG-IgA > 10 x normal with a positive endomysial antibody in a second blood sample who do not undergo EGD with biopsies

10. Multiple duodenal biopsies recommended for diagnosis in both adults and children
    - 4 in distal duodenum, 1-2 in the bulb

11. Celiac disease associated with
    - Microscopic colitis
    - Dermatitis herpetiformis
    - Hypothyroidism, DM
    - Selective IgA deficiency
    - Increased liver function tests, Primary biliary cholangitis (PBC)
    - GERD, EoE

- Pancreatitis, Cardiomyopathy, Female reproductive issues

12. Dermatitis herpetiformis is associated with celiac disease
    - Pruritic papulovescicular rash on extensor surfaces of elbows, knes, buttocks and scalp
    - Granular linear deposition of IgA along dermo-epidermal junction
    - Treated with Dapsone

13. Well controlled celiac disease with ongoing diarrhea, consider microscopic colitis as a possible cause of symptoms
    - Colonoscopy with biopsies

14. Gluten free Oats are a safe part of gluten free diet

15. Buckwheat is gluten free

16. Gluten free diet is
    - Higher in fat, Calorees
    - Lower in proteins and fiber
    - Low vitamin B, Ca, folate, vitamin A , Mg and Fe
    - More expensive and more likely to gain weight

17. Adults to receive PCV20 for pneumococcal vaccine initially at diagnosis and booster at age 65 years
    - However, ACG 2023 recommends vaccination for adults > 65, smokers between 19-64 and adults with certain conditions
    - If PCV 15 vaccine is used, follow a year later with PCV23 vaccine

18. Lymphocytic duodenosis (>25 lymphocytes per HPF) not specific for celiac disease

19. Intestinal healing is the goal of gluten free diet
    - Standard of care in diet adherence involves visiting a dietitian with expertise in GFD

20. Lack of response or relapse of symptoms
    - EGD with biopsies

21. Asymptomatic celiac disease, repeat EGD with biopsies 2 years after starting gluten free diet

22. No role for gluten detection devices in food
    - Dysbiosis is a part of celiac disease
    - Probiotics have not demonstrated benefits

23. Case finding in celiac disease. Consider testing
   - All first degree relatives of confirmed celiac disease with or without signs, symptoms or abnormal labs
   - Patients with malabsorption
   - Down's syndrome
   - No role for community/ mass testing for celiac disease

24. Fe deficiency with negative EGD
   - Check for TTG
   - Check for celiac disease when anemia is associated with abnormal liver enzymes

Refractory Celiac Disease

1. Older patient with celiac disease with unresponsive symptoms
   - Long scope enteroscopy
   - Due to risk of strictures avoid video capsule
   - r/o ulcerative jejunoileitis and enteropathy associated T cell lymphomas

2. Elderly patients with celiac disease that stops responding to diet (refractory) and now has intraepithelial lymphocytes carry poor prognosis

3. Types of refractory celiac disease
   - Type 1 refractory celiac disease is characterized by a normal intraepithelial lymphocyte population
   - Type 2 is defined by the presence of an aberrant, clonal intraepithelial lymphocyte population.

4. CTE or MRE or video capsule to exclude enteropathy-associated T-cell lymphoma and ulcerative jejunoileitis at initial diagnosis of type 2 refractory celiac disease

5. Celiac disease associated with Non-Hodgkin's B/T cell lymphoma and small bowel adenocarcinoma
   - Enteropathic T cell lymphoma has low CD8 cells
     - Associated with dermatitis herpetiformis and chronic intermittent adherence to gluten free diet
     - May present with multifocal perforations of the gut
     - T cell lymphomas express CD3 and CD7
     - Jejum is the commonest site
   - Breast cancer is reduced in celiac disease

6. Refractory Celiac disease (AGA 2022)
   - Check all evidence of celiac disease: serological, endoscopic and histological
   - Check for ongoing gluten exposure by serologic testing, dietitian review, detection of immunogenic peptides in urine and stools
   - EGD with biopsies to look for villous atrophy
   - Consider other causes of villous atrophy, including CVID, autoimmune enteropathy, tropical sprue and medication-induced enteropathy.
   - After exclusion of gluten, r/o other causes including Microscopic colitis, Pancreatic insufficiency, IBD, Lactose or fructose intolerance and Small intestinal bacterial overgrowth (SIBO)
   - Flow cytometry, immunohistochemistry to look for subtypes of refractory celiac disease and T-cell lymphoma
   - Detailed nutritional assessment

7. Refractory celiac disease, findings on previous small bowel biopsy should be reviewed as a priority

8. Albumin is a prognostic factor in refractory celiac disease
   - Correct deficiencies
   - Parenteral nutrition in severe malnutrition

9. Budesonide or prednisone are first-line therapy in either type 1 or type 2 refractory celiac disease

10. Other causes of villous atrophy without celiac disease include CVID, autoimmune enteritis, tropical sprue and medication induced sprue

Other Malabsorptive Disorders

1. D-xylose test
   - Normal test indicates normal small bowel and kidney function
   - Normal in chronic pancreatitis

2. Olmesartan may mimic celiac disease with villous atrophy. *Absence of DQ2/ DQ8 rules out celiac disease*
   - Also presents with collagen band ~ 3 years after initiation

3. Whipple's disease affects mainly middle aged male Caucasians with exposure to soils or animals
   - May present as fever of unknown origin
   - Cardinal symptoms are arthralgias, weight loss, diarrhea and abdominal pain
       - Arthalgias preceding onset of malabsorbtion
   - Neurological symptoms such as Ophthalmoplegia, myoclonus, dementia
       - Occulomasticatory myorhythmia is pathognomonic
   - GI symptoms > neurological symptoms
   - Pericarditis, arthritis, lymphadenopathy, chronic cough with pleural effusions
   - Normal celiac disease serology
   - Abnormal d-xylose test
   - Occult GI bleed in 20-30 %
   - *Small bowel biopsies with PAS+ Macrophages in lamina propria*
   - Ceftriaxone induction x 2 weeks followed by longer term treatment with Bactrim.
   - In Sulfa allergy, use Doxycycline and hydroxychloroquine but CNS penetrance can be limited and requires treatment with Ceftriaxone

4. Autoimmune enteritis
   - *Like celiac disease but withOUT Intra epithelial lymphocytes (IEL) and Celiac serology negative*
   - Check for anti-enterocyte antibody or anti-goblet cell antibody
   - Apoptotic bodies within crypts
   - Low number of or absent goblet cells, Paneth cells
   - Associated with other autoimmune diseases such as MS or RA
   - Treat with prednisone/ infliximab

5. Common variable immunodeficiency (CVID) presents with malabsorption
   - Associated with diarrhea, abdominal pain, weight loss, sinus infections and bronchitis

- Low IgA levels
- Infection of GI, sinus or respiratory system
- High risk of giardia, salmonella, norovirus and campylobacter
    - Recurrent giardia infection
    - Increased stool alpha 1 antitrypsin levels
    - Immunoglobulin panel that would show low immunoglobins
- Duodenal biopsies show villous atrophy and lymphocyte invasion with follicular lymphoid hyperplasia and *low/no plasma cells*
- Colon biopsy show increased CD8 T cell infiltration of colon
- Diagnosed through quantitative immunoglobulin assay
- Budesonide or systemic steroids, IVIG of limited use

6. In agammaglobulinemia, there are no plasma cells in the villi

7. Abetalipoproteinemia shows vacuolated villi on histology

8. Collagenous sprue with a collagen band (10 microns wide), treated with corticosteroids/ Budesonide but doesn't respond to gluten free diet

9. Infections may lead to post infectious IBS

10. Intestinal lymphangiectasia caused by
    - Malignancy, thoracic duct obstruction
    - Right heart failure, Cirrhosis, Mesenteric venous thrombosis
    - Crohn's, Sarcoidosis, TB, Whipple's disease
    - Congenital syndromes such as von Recklinghausen, Turner (X0) or Noonan, Klippel-Trenaunay and Hennekam

11. Intestinal lymphangiectasia presents with hypoalbuminemia, pedal edema, malnutrition
    - *Increased A1AT levels in stools indicating protein loss*
    - Therapy is with medium chain triglycerides that is absorbed directly into portal vein bypassing lymphatics

12. Commonest site of amyloidosis in GI tract is descending duodenum followed by colorectal and esophagus
    - Pink amorphous mucosal deposits on histology
    - Primary amyloidosis is associated with underlying malignancy- affects mucosa, submucosa and musclaris
    - Secondary amyloidosis is associated with underlying chronic inflammation such as ankylosing spondilitis and affects mucosa

13. Fat malabsorption causes oxalate kidney stones due to dietary calcium binding to fat rather than oxalates

Short Bowel Syndrome

1. Small bowel resection has increased risk of *oxalate stones*
   - Small bowel resection with right flank pain scenario
   - Reduce oxalate in the diet
   - *Increase calcium in the diet which binds to oxalate*
   - Oxalosis reduced by potassium citrate and calcium

2. TI resection and steatorrhea
   - Up to 100 cm of TI resection causes bile acid diarrhea treated with cholestyramine
   - >100 cm of ileal resection causes steatorrhea and bile salt loss. Treat with low fat diet and medium chain triglycerides
   - Cholestyramine (Questran) and URSO worsen diarrhea in TI resection > 100 cm
   - Fat is absorbed via lymphatics/thoracic duct and not portal vein
        - Medium chain triglycerides are absorbed into the portal vein
   - Ileum can resume jejunal function but not vice versa. Jejunum resection has no sequelae since ileum can take over
   - Loss of ileum needs replacement of B12, selenium and fat soluble vitamins

3. Teduglutide (Gaffex) is a GLP2 agonist
   - Increased height of villi
   - Reduced gastric emptying
   - Reduces TPN in small intestinal failure

4. Predictive of long term TPN in short gut syndrome
   - < 50 cm of small bowel + colon
   - < 100-150 cm without colon
   - Older age
   - Residual disease
   - Fasting plasma citrulline < 20

5. Short bowel syndrome (SBS) (AGA 2022)
   - Serum vitamin and trace element concentrations should be measured at baseline and monitored annually
   - Most favorable anatomy is Type 3 (Jejunoileocolic) and least favorable is Type 1 (End jejunostomy)

6. Vitamin D levels checked through serum 25-hydroxyvitamin D and parathyroid hormone

7. SBS with colon need a high-carbohydrate (60%), low-fat (20%).
   - End-jejunostomy does not benefit from fat restriction
   - Oxalate restriction (eg, peanuts and baked beans) in those with a colon who are at risk of hyperoxaluria and oxalate stones

8. Parenteral nutrition (PN) in SBS
   - > 50% weaned off PN, most within 2 years of surgery
   - Tunneled central catheter preferred over peripheral catheter and ports

9. Oral rehydration solution
   - End jejunostomy need ORS isotonic solution
   - SBS with a colon can tolerate hypotonic solutions

10. Pharmacologic therapy of SBS
    - PPIs and H2RAs reduce gastric secretion and acid effect on pancreatic enzymes and intestinal mucosa
    - Octreotide only in difficult large volume stool losses
       - Avoid Octreotide during the intestinal adaptation phase
    - Antidiarrheals may also reduce intestinal secretion
    - Transdermal clonidine reduces motility and secretion
    - No Bile salt binders (Steatorrhea if > 100 cm TI is lost)
    - Teduglutide is a GLP2 analogue
       - Never in recent (< 5 years) history of ANY malignancy
       - Baseline colonoscopy needed
    - Surgery lengthening and reconstructive operations
    - Potassium citrate and calcium to reduce Oxalosis
    - Intestinal transplantation

11. Antidiarrheals in SBS
    - Loperamide and codeine may have synergistic effect
    - Loperamide preferred over opiates (Diphenoxylate) due to lower risks
    - Large doses (16 tabs/32 mg/day) of loperamide may be needed due to loss of enterohepatic circulation

12. In short gut syndrome ideal oral rehydrating solution should be isotonic high sodium: glucose ratio

13. Surgery lengthening procedures in SBS
    - Longitudinal intestinal lengthening and tapering (LILT) operation by Bianchi and Serial transverse enteroplasty (STEP) operation by Kim
    - No critical differences in outcomes between the 2 main lengthening operations

14. Intestinal transplantation in SBS 65% 5 year survival
    - Refractory TPN dependency and associated liver failure

- Complications of TPN such as thrombosis of central veins
- 50% needed Liver transplantation at the same time
- T bili has to be < 4.5 mg /dl
- Early transplant in Desmoid tumors, Dysmotility syndrome and TPN dependence

GI Bleed

1. Aortoenteric fistula needs an emergent CT scan/ CT angiogram

2. Obscure GI bleed from small bowel
   - Small bowel tumors more common in younger people < 40 years of age
   - Arteriovenous malformation (AVM) more common in older people
      - Associated with aortic stenosis and chronic kidney disease
   - Celiac disease and NSAIDS at any age
   - Treat with thalidomide and octreotide

3. Heyde's syndrome
   - Aortic stenosis, acquired von WIllebrand syndrome and intestinal angiodysplasias

4. Meckel's diverticulum
   - Causes obscure GI bleed in younger individuals
   - Ectopic gastric mucosa or pancreatic tissue and can cause ulcers
   - Detected by Technetium 99m pertechnetate scan

SIBO

1. Folate levels increased and B12 decreased in small bowel bacterial overgrowth (SIBO)

2. Most common symptom of SIBO is bloating (ACG 2020)
  - Vitamin deficiency is uncommon and may occur in iatrogenic or structural abnormalities of the small bowel
  - Test for suspected SIBO is GLUCOSE (or lactulose) hydrogen breath test in IBS patients, symptomatic patients with small bowel motility issues or prior abdominal surgery
    - Correct dose for breath testing is 75 g of Glucose or 10 g of lactulose
    - Breath test is not a good test for SIBO and can be affected by smoking, oral intake and physical activity
    - Glucose hydrogen breath test is negative if < 20 ppm above baseline in 90 minutes
  - Colony count of greater than 10^3 CFU/ml is consistent with SIBO
  - Treat symptomatic SIBO with antibiotics (ACG 2020)
    - Rifaximin (drug of choice) and Neomycin
  - FMT or probiotics not recommended
  - Prevent SIBO by avoiding multiple courses of antibiotics

3. Severe cases of bacterial overgrowth leading to liver failure or recurrent sepsis may warrant intestinal transplantation

4. Hydrogen breath test showing 2 peaks of H2 > 12ppm in SIBO
  - Early peak on lactulose breath test is SIBO (can be caused by Crohn's disease with fistula)
  - Associated with Chronic pancreatitis, Crohn's disease (CD), Scleroderma and Hypothyroidism

5. Megaduodenum associated with scleroderma and SIBO
  - Positive ANA and anti-topoisomerase 1 Ab

6. ANNA1 and ANNA2 antibody associated with paraneoplastic visceral neuropathy associated with small cell lung cancer
  - Person with erythema on cheeks, lung findings and low B12 has scleroderma with SIBO

7. Test for methane with glucose or lactulose breath test for intestinal methanogen overgrowth in symptomatic patients with *constipation* (ACG 2020)
  - Methanobrevibacter smithi is a key methanogen

8. Long term immunosuppression is a risk for small bowel bacterial overgrowth

Ischemia

1. Henoch Schoenlein purpura
    - Self-limited, autoimmune complex small vessel vasculitis with multiorgan involvement
    - Classic triad of nonthrombocytopenic purpura, arthritis, GI/ renal involvement
    - Abdominal pain, joint pains, fever, sore throat, erythematous and non-pruritic rash on extremities, hematuria, watery diarrhea, elevated CRP, increased WBC, terminal ileitis in young patients.
    - GI involvement may mimic Crohn's disease (CD)
    - Biopsies show leukocytoclastic vasculitis in TI and skin.
    - Treated with prednisone x 12 weeks. If steroids not helpful then immunosuppressive drug such as cyclophosphamide, Azathioprine (Imuran), cyclosporine A and mycophenolate with IV high dose pulse steroids

2. Middle aged with hx of MI, hypotension, abdominal pain and mesenteric ischemia
    - Non-occlusive ischemia
    - CT of the abdomen and pelvis to rule out other causes

3. Mesenteric arterial occlusive disease
    - First symptom of mesenteric ischemia is abdominal pain disproportionate to tenderness
    - May present with intermittent pain for several months followed by worsening
    - Atrial fibrillation with sudden onset abdominal pain is SMA thrombus
    - SMA atherosclerotic plaque that evolves into complete thrombosis
    - Focal segmental ischemia evolves into mesenteric ischemia
    - CT angiogram. Doppler ultrasound in patients with elevated creatinine

4. Target or donut sign is enteroenteric intussusception - refer to surgery

5. Chronic mesenteric ischemia presents with weight loss, periumbilical pain and fear of eating (sitophobia)
    - CT imaging often shows stenosis of SMA

Neoplasms

1. Obscure GI bleed with ileal neoplasm with histopathology showing solid blue cells, diagnosis is carcinoid and check for chromogranin A

2. GIST is the commonest tumor of the small bowel in neurofibromatosis

3. Octreotide in carcinoid syndrome controls tumor bulk and symptoms

4. Small bowel tumors more common in younger people < 40 years of age

5. Non-Hodgkin's lymphoma affecting the HIV patients would be of B cell variety
   - Non-Hodgkin's lymphoma affecting the small bowel in celiac disease is of T cell variety

6. Incurable malignant GOO undergoing palliative intervention, either SEMS placement or surgical GJ (ASGE 2020)
   - SEMS in poor surgical candidates with short life expectancy (<6 months) and those who place a high value on resumption of oral diet and being discharged early
   - Surgery in patients with a life expectancy of >6 months and good performance status
   - Covered SEMS is equivalent to uncovered SEMS.

7. Insufficient evidence to support endoscopic management over surgical management in Benign GOO (ASGE 2020)

8. Surveillance of duodenal adenomas based on Spigelman staging which is an elaborate point system based on the number of polyps, size, histology and presence of dysplasia
   - Stage 0 (no polyps) q3-5 years
   - Stage 1 (1-4 points) q2-3 years
   - Stage 2 (5-6 points) q1-2 years
   - Stage 3 (7-8 points) q6-12 months
   - Stage 4 (9-12 points): in the absence of duodenectomy q3-6 months

9. Endoscopic therapy for ampullary adenomas
   - Size < 3 cm
   - Ingrowth into CBD or PD < 2 cm
   - Absence of advanced duodenal polyposis (Spiegelman stage 4)

10. When ampulla has ca in situ, recommend surgical resection

11. CT enterography is superior to video capsule to detect small bowel masses

12. VIPoma, causes WDHA syndrome
    - Watery diarrhea
    - Dehydration
    - Hypokalemia
    - Achlorhydria

13. Small bowel carcinoids arise from enterochromaffin cells in the crypts of Lieberkuhn
    - Early mets in lesions < 2 cm
    - Most common small bowel tumors
    - Survival data is better for NET than adenocarcinomas

4. COLON

Defecatory Disorders

1. Defecation process
   - Abdominal wall contracts
   - Internal anal sphincter (IS) and puborectalis relax
   - Widening of anorectal angle
   - External anal sphincter (ES) relaxes
   - Perineum descends
     - Dyssynergia if the above doesn't happen

2. Defecatory disorders (DD)
   - Digital rectal examination for initial evaluation is strongly recommended
   - Initial approach is normalizing stool form, evacuation toilet position and behavior
   - Anorectal manometry (ARM) and balloon expulsion test (BET) are required to diagnose defecatory disorders
   - Predicts outcome and guides biofeedback therapy

3. Symptoms include
   - Manual maneuvers to facilitate evacuation
   - Excessive straining
   - Sense of anorectal blockage
   - Sense of incomplete evacuation

4. Rectal intussusception is where a bulge is felt at the tip of the finger while bearing down

5. Coccydynia is when tenderness is noted on palpating coccyx

6. A defect or dip anteriorly felt by digital rectal exam while patient is straining is a Rectocele

7. False positives can occur with ARM. Results of various anorectal tests may disagree

8. Normal anal sphincter resting pressure is 60 mm of Hg, squeeze is > 120 mm

9. Anorectal manometry and balloon expulsion test for those who fail OTC laxatives and fiber supplements
   - Dyssynergic defecation is > 2 minutes to expel balloon with defecation (Balloon expulsion normally <1 minute)

- Manometry with balloon expulsion may show a U-shaped high-pressure area in pelvic floor dysfunction
- Secretagogues and prokinetic medications only after anorectal manometry

10. Rectal manometry doesn't assess puborectalis muscle. Only digital rectal examination assesses it

11. Distension of the rectum causes rectal inhibitory reflex (RAIR) which involves relaxation of internal anal sphincter
    - If recto-anal inhibitory reflex (RAIR) is absent in response to balloon distension, consider deep rectal biopsies to r/o Hirschsprung's disease

12. Anal examination good for testing resting and squeeze function accurately
    - Anal pressures should be compared only with normal values of the same age and sex cohort

13. Defecography should not be performed before ARM and a rectal balloon expulsion test (AGA 2013). Defecography doesn't detect colon transit
    - Colonic transit study only after normal ARM and failure of secretagogues/prokinetic medications or failure of treatment of defecatory disorders
    - *Colonoscopy not required for constipation* outside of age-appropriate screening or alarm symptoms

14. Defecography needed in patients with defecatory disorders who fail conservative management and biofeedback
    - Most patients with structural abnormalities do not require surgery (ACG 2021)

15. Pelvic floor dysfunctions/ defecatory disorders need *pelvic floor retraining and biofeedback*

16. Change in bowel habits with incontinence
    - Colonoscopy needed
    - Anorectal manometry (ARM)- sphincter dysfunction
    - EUS-R for sphincter defects
    - Digital rectal examination for resting tone, sphincter squeeze, skin tags, scar, fissures etc.
    - CT scan not required

17. Fecal incontinence
    - Conservative management and biofeedback

- If associated with diarrhea, treat with antidiarrheals
- Barrier agents such as anal plugs or Bulking agents such as dextranomer sodium considered in patient who fail to respond to conservative management with low anal sphincter resting pressure and low anal squeeze pressure
- Sacral nerve stimulation (SNS) in those who fail to respond
- SNS improves fecal incontinence
- Sphincteroplasty in patients with acute anal sphincter injuries
- Offer end-stoma to patients with severe fecal incontinence that fails to respond to other therapy

18. Pudendal neuropathy
    - Rectal sensation normal
    - Anal resting pressure normal
    - Anal squeeze weak
    - Intact IS and ES on EUS
    - Pudendal nerve testing (PNTML) not accurate for pudendal neuropathy
    - Both sensation and squeeze is low then Multiple sclerosis or spinal tumor
        - Anal wink reflex is absent

19. Scleroderma
    - Normal rectal sensation
    - Reduced resting anal pressure due to IS dysfunction
    - Normal squeeze
    - Intact IS on US

20. Birthing injury reduces squeeze due to ES dysfunction
    - Multiple sclerosis (MS) causes reduced squeeze and reduced sensations

21. Fecal incontinence with 15% defect in external anal sphincter, treatment is sacral nerve stimulation. Sphincteroplasty not helpful

22. Anal fissure
    - Rectal manometry shows anal sphincter hypertonia
    - Usually seen in the posterior midline
        - 25% in anterior midline
    - Atypical appearance raises a concern for infections and IBD
    - Chronic anal fissure lasts > 8-12 weeks and has edema + fibrosis

23. Treatment of anal fissure is softening stools and relaxing sphincter pressure to improve perfusion
    - Trial of medical management prior to surgery referral
    - Calcium channel blocker, Botox injection and in resistant cases surgical

treatment with sphincterotomy (not sphincteroplasty which is for incontinence)
- If patient is at a low risk of incontinence, then lateral sphincterotomy
- If patient is at a high risk of incontinence, then Botox or fissurectomy

24. Colonic transit normal if 80% of markers have passed by day 5
- Slow transit constipation if > 20% of markers present
- If all markers are in the rectosigmoid then evaluate for colonic outlet obstruction via anorectal manometry

25. Treatment of choice for refractory slow transit constipation (STC) without defecatory disorder is subtotal colectomy with ileorectal anastomosis (IRA)
- Colonic intraluminal testing (manometry, barostat) should be considered to document colonic motor dysfunction before colectomy

26. Normal transit constipation (NTC) and STC can be safely managed with long-term use of laxatives

27. Suppositories or enemas rather than oral laxatives alone should be considered in patients with refractory pelvic floor dysfunction

28. Constipation in pregnancy - treat with fiber

29. Kegel's exercise has the same efficacy as pelvic floor retraining for fecal incontinence
- Continence improves in 80-90% after surgery but deteriorates over time

30. Hirschsprung's disease
- Male
- Internal sphincter (IS) denervated and doesn't relax with rectal distension
- Ganglion cells absent
- Full thickness rectal biopsies show **increased** Acetylcholinesterase staining

31. Full thickness rectal prolapse needs surgery (abdominal rectopexy or in select cases perianal procedures- ACG 2021)

32. Chronic proctalgia syndrome lasts for at least 20 minutes and other causes needs to be ruled out
- Levator syndrome has levator tenderness
- Levator tenderness absent in proctalgia syndrome

- DRE and history enough to diagnose proctalgia syndrome
- Treated by biofeedback and galvanic stimulation. No role for Botox or massage

33. Proctalgia fugax lasts less than 20 minutes
- Reassurance and explanation of syndrome is enough. No intervention needed
- Anorectal conditions such as hemorrhoids or fissure doesn't rule out proctalgia fugax

Polyps

1. Colorectal cancer (CRC) screening (AGA 2021)
    - Strongly recommendation for CRC screening ages 50 to 75
    - Suggests CRC screening in average-risk individuals ages 45-49
    - Ages 76 to 85, screening individualize
    - Screening is not recommended after age 85.
    - Polyps in 30% of males and 20% of females- Adenoma detection rate (ADR) ≥30% in men and ≥20% in women (AGA 2020)

2. CRC risk has increased in 45- to 49-year-olds over the past 20 years

3. Colonoscopy rather than non-invasive tests for 45-50 years old who are at higher risk for advanced adenomas
    - Current smoking
    - Obesity
    - Low levels of physical activity

4. Multi-target stool (mts) DNA for screening q 3 years

5. If 2 first degree relatives at any age or one FDR with Colorectal cancer (CRC) or advanced polyp < 60 years, colonoscopy q 5 years
    - First degree relatives of patients with advanced lesions need to have colonoscopy (and not alternative screening)
    - First degree relative with CRC (or significant adenoma) < 60 years is colonoscopy 10 years younger than the index and then every 5 years

6. One second degree relative with CRC has no increased risk of CRC

7. FIT is less sensitive but MORE specific than MTsDNA (Cologuard).
    - MTsDNA is approved only in average-risk adults aged 45–85 years
        - More sensitive but less specific than FIT

8. Mailed FIT test increases CRC screening rates
    - Offering a choice of stool test or colonoscopy increases the screening rates
    - If positive, colonoscopy within 2 months

9. Recommend FIT over FOBT for CRC screening due to increased sensitivity (AGA 2016)
    - A positive FIT and a negative colonoscopy should not prompt UGI evaluation.
    - FIT screening programs rely on spontaneously passed stool specimens

and not an in-office digital rectal examination (DRE) sample

10. Methylated septin 9 DNA blood test has > 99% negative predictive value for CRC. False +ve in other cancers. False negative in CAD/ DM
   - The Septin 9 blood test is FDA (but not Medicare)-approved serum test for CRC screening
   - Septin 9 not recommended for screening

11. FIT q1y and colonoscopy q10y primary modality for screening (ACG 2021)
   - Flexible sigmoidoscopy q5-10y, multitarget stool DNA q3y, CT colonography q5y and colon capsule q5y are alternates

12. Co-pays and deductibles are barriers to screening and contribute to socioeconomic disparities. (AGA 2022)

13. AICD inactivated prior to polyp removal
   - Polyp with AICD consult a cardiologist

14. Small polyp- remove by cold snare / large capacity forceps (AGA recommends only cold snares for 3 mm or larger polyps)

15. Incomplete polypectomy on biopsy but complete endoscopically, repeat colon in 6 months
   - Piecemeal resection, repeat colon 6-12 months

16. Traditional serrated adenomas need colonoscopy every 3 years

17. Tubulovillous (TV) adenoma - return in 3 years

18. Colonoscopy in patients with peritoneal dialysis treat with Ampicillin 1 gm IV and single dose aminoglycoside

19. Ulcerative colitis (UC)+ Primary sclerosing cholangitis (PSC) patients after liver transplantation need colonoscopy every year

20. In patients with metastatic CRC, surgery of primary tumor only with bleeding or impending obstruction

21. Sessile serrated adenoma is a marker for synchronous colorectal adenomas

22. Incremental effectiveness of repeat colonoscopy after baseline normal colonoscopy for further reducing CRC incidence and mortality is uncertain

(AGA 2020)

23. Surveillance colonoscopy after baseline removal of adenoma with high-risk features (eg, size ≥10 mm) may reduce risk for incident CRC, but impact on fatal CRC is uncertain. (AGA 2020)
  - Normal, high-quality colonoscopy, repeat CRC screening in 10 years.

24. 1–2 tubular adenomas <10 mm in size completely removed at a high-quality examination, repeat colonoscopy in 7–10 years
  - 3–4 tubular adenomas <10 mm in size completely removed at a high-quality examination, repeat colonoscopy in 3–5 years, if normal at that time, then subsequent colonoscopy in 10 years
  - 5–10 tubular adenomas <10 mm in size completely removed at a high-quality examination, repeat colonoscopy in 3 years
  - 1 or more adenomas ≥10 mm in size completely removed at high-quality examination, repeat colonoscopy in 3 years
    - After 2 colonoscopies with low risk, subsequent colonoscopies at 10 years
  - Adenoma containing high-grade dysplasia completely removed at high-quality examination, repeat colonoscopy in 3 years
  - >10 adenomas completely removed at high-quality examination, repeat colonoscopy in 1 year

25. Patients with <20 hyperplastic polyps (HPs) <10 mm in size in the rectosigmoid colon or proximal colon removed at a high-quality examination, repeat CRC screening in 10 years

26. 1–2 sessile serrated polyps (SSPs) <10 mm in size completely removed at high-quality examination, repeat colonoscopy in 5–10 years
  - 3–4 SSPs <10 mm at high-quality examination, repeat colonoscopy in 3–5 years
  - SSP ≥10 mm at a high-quality examination, repeat colonoscopy in 3 years. If 2 or more > 10 mm then repeat in 1 year
  - For patients with HP ≥10 mm, repeat colonoscopy in 3–5 years
  - SSP containing dysplasia at a high-quality examination, repeat colonoscopy in 3 years

27. Bowel prep score < 6 is associated with future risk of colorectal neoplasia

28. Photo documentation of all lesions ≥10 mm in size before removal, and suggest photo documentation of the post-resection defect

29. Cold snare polypectomy to remove diminutive (≤5 mm) and small (6–9 mm) lesions due to high complete resection rates and safety profile

- No cold forceps polypectomy to remove diminutive (≤5 mm) lesions due to high rates of incomplete resection
- Cold biopsies (jumbo or large capacity) to remove polyps only < 2 mm
- No hot biopsy forceps for polypectomy of diminutive (≤5 mm) and small (6–9 mm) lesions

30. For polyps < 1 cm, cold snare polypectomy has lower risk of bleed

31. EMR as the preferred treatment method of large (≥20 mm) non-pedunculated colorectal lesions. (AGA 2020)
    - Snare resection of all visible tissue of a lesion in one colonoscopy session
    - Indigo carmine or methylene blue, in the submucosal injection solution to facilitate recognition of the submucosa from the mucosa and muscularis propria layers.
    - No tattoo, using sterile carbon particle suspension, as the submucosal injection solution.
    - Use viscous injection solution for lesions ≥20 mm to remove the lesion in fewer pieces and less procedure time compared to normal saline.
    - Do NOT use ablative techniques (APC, snare tip soft coagulation) on endoscopically visible residual tissue of a lesion
    - Use adjuvant thermal ablation of the post-EMR margin, where no endoscopically visible adenoma remains despite meticulous inspection

32. Prophylactic closure of resection defects ≥20 mm in size in the right colon, when closure is feasible.
    - No benefits to prophylactic coagulation of blood vessels
    - Prophylactic mechanical ligation of the stalk with a detachable loop or clips on pedunculated lesions with head ≥20 mm or with stalk thickness ≥5 mm to reduce post-polypectomy bleeding.

33. CRC/ Advanced polyp < 60 years or 2 FDR with CRC or Advanced polyps at any age (ACG 2021)
    - Colon at age 40 and q5y
    - CRC/Advanced polyp in 1 FDR> 60 years then colon at age 40 and resume average risk screening (ACG 2021)

34. All endoscopists should measure ADR, Cecal intubation rate (>95%) and withdrawal times (> 6 minutes) (ACG 2021)

35. Cold or hot snare polypectomies of sessile polyps 10-19 mm (ACG 2020)
    - Hot snare of pedunculated polyps > 10 mm

36. CO_2 preferred instead of air for Colonoscopy or EMR

37. Restart anticoagulation on the day of the EMR procedure

37. Endoscopic mucosal dissection for large polyp recurrence after an EMR
    - Also, for T1a cancerous polyp
    - T1b polyp management is surgery

38. Endoscopic full thickness dissection not recommended for polyps > 2.5 cm in the colon

39. Small colonic perforation (5 mm or less) can be managed by through the scope endoscopic clips, confirming CO_2 and keeping the perforated site in a non-water dependent position

40. Prolapse type polyps associated with fibromuscular hyperplasia, extension of muscularis mucosae into lamina propria and crypt elongation

Colorectal Cancer (CRC)

1. Chemoprevention in CRC
   - Low dose aspirin to reduce CRC incidence and mortality if < 70 years, 10% Cardiovascular risk, not at high risk of bleeding and life expectancy of at least 10 years
   - Aspirin to prevent recurrent colorectal neoplasia among individuals with CRC history
   - Metformin to reduce mortality in concurrent DM2 and CRC
   - Metformin in Type 2 DM to prevent Colorectal neoplasia

2. Patient with rectal cancer and transanal resection
   - Increased risk of local recurrence
       - Transanal resection
       - Surgery without total mesorectal excision
       - Lack of neoadjuvant therapy followed by surgery with mesorectal excision
   - Flexible sigmoidoscopy or EUS every 3-6 months for the first 2-3 years after surgery. These surveillance measures are in addition to recommended colonoscopic surveillance for metachronous neoplasia

3. CRC with favorable data
   - Invasion depth < 1000 mc
   - En bloc resection
   - Well to moderately differentiated
   - Clear resection margin
   - No lymphovascular invasion

4. Cancerous polyp with unfavorable histology
   - Depth > 1 mm
   - Poor differentiation - Poor differentiation of cancerous polyp needs surgical resection
   - Lymphovascular invasion
   - Distance < 1 mm from resection margin
   - Tumor budding

5. Large laterally spreading tumor in the cecum
   - Decreased cancer risk
   - Reduced submucosal fibrosis risk
   - NICE 3 or Kudo 4 associated with submucosal invasion
   - IC valve involvement treat with EMR
   - Appendix involvement cannot be treated with EMR
   - T1a lesion can be managed by ESD

6. EUS guided biopsy of a solid lesion such as perirectal lymph node (LN) in Rectal cancer
   - No antibiotics

7. Stage 4 CRC in elderly people- Chemotherapy discussion and referral

8. Treatment of CRC with solitary liver metastasis is surgery

9. African Americans have worse outcomes with CRC
   - Alaskan natives have 2 x risk of CRC

10. Pedunculated and non-pedunculated polyps with NICE classification type 3 or Kudo classification of type V be considered to have deep submucosal invasion
    - Non pedunculated lesions with these features should be biopsied (in the area of surface feature disruption), tattooed (unless in or near the cecum), and referred to surgery
    - Tattoo placed 3-5 cm distally to the lesion
    - Pedunculated polyps with features of deep submucosal invasion should undergo endoscopic polypectomy.

11. Increased risk of submucosally invasive cancer in
    - Laterally Spreading Tumor: non-granular (LST-NG) morphology with sessile shape or depression
    - Laterally Spreading Tumor-Granular (LST-G) with a dominant nodule
    - En bloc endoscopic resection, instead of piecemeal resection. In the case of LST-G with a dominant nodule, at least the nodular area should be considered for en bloc resection.
    - All pedunculated polyps, even if large, should be resected en bloc.

12. Patients with CRC undergo high-quality perioperative clearing with colonoscopy preoperatively, or within a 3- to 6-month interval after surgery in the case of obstructive CRC. (AGA 2016)
    - First surveillance colonoscopy 1 year after surgery or 1 year after the clearing perioperative colonoscopy
    - In patients with obstructive CRC precluding complete colonoscopy, CTC to exclude synchronous neoplasms. Double-contrast barium enema is an acceptable alternative

13. Anal squamous cell cancer- management by colorectal surgeon
    - Rectal cancer doesn't arise from anal verge
    - Imiquimod is the therapy for anal condylomas
    - Associated with HPV 16 and 18

- HPV 6 and 11 associated with condylomata

14. Gay HIV+ men are at high risk and benefit from digital anorectal examination with anal cytology and high resolution anoscopy with Lugol's iodine and acetic acid

15. Patient with HIV and squamous cells ca of the anal canal, refer to chemoradiation

16. Rectal carcinoid
    - If > 1.5 cm = 25% metastasis
    - > 2 cm then 100% metastases
    - Only 30% have carcinoid syndrome with flushing, diarrhea
    - < 1.5 cm is usually asymptomatic and no need for 5 HIAA

17. Cetuximab and panitumumab are EGFR inhibitors
    - Bevacizumab impedes tumor angiogenesis via VEGF pathway
        - Also used for resistant AVM's

18. Rectal bleed at any age is a red flag symptom and needs colonoscopy

Polyposis Syndrome

1. Lynch, Familial adenomatous polyposis (FAP), Juvenile Polyposis syndrome are all autosomal dominant (AD)
     - MUTYH or MYH associated polyposis (MAP), a form of mismatch repair gene, is autosomal recessive (AR)

2. Genetic counseling for
     - Patients with 10 or more adenomas found on a single endoscopy and 20 or more adenomas during their lifetime (ASGE 2020)
     - First-degree relatives of confirmed polyposis syndrome patients
     - Patients with 10-100 polyps need to be evaluated for attenuated FAP or MYH associated polyposis (MAP)

3. Polyposis screening in FAP (ASGE 2020)
     - Screening sigmoidoscopy or colonoscopy in children suspected to have FAP starting at ages 10 to 12 years.
     - Attenuated FAP (AFAP) or MAP screening colonoscopy at age 18-20
     - Sigmoidoscopy in patients with ileorectal anastomosis (IRA) surgery at 6-month to 1-year intervals indefinitely
     - Celecoxib and sulindac have demonstrated chemoprevention in FAP

4. FAP and UGI surveillance
     - Random biopsy and targeted biopsy sampling of any suspicious lesions to assess for dysplasia and accurate duodenal Spigelman stage (SS) in FAP
     - SS is based on polyp numbers, size, histology and presence of dysplasia
     - Baseline SS ≥7 is associated with the development of duodenal HGD.
     - EGD done q2-3 years for SS2
     - SS4 is q 3-6 months or refer to surgery

5. Endoscopic resection of gastric and duodenal polyps >1 cm
     - Endoscopic resection of all antral polyps, given the predominance of gastric adenomas in this location
     - Careful examination of the ampulla and periampullary region using a duodenoscope or cap-assisted gastroscope. Biopsy only if mucosal abnormality present
     - EGD only after the age of 25 years
     - Gastric cancer risk is low

6. FAP and other organ systems
     - Increased risk of Thyroid cancer, Thyroid ultrasound annually
     - No increased risk of GYN tumors
     - Congenital hypertrophy of retinal pigmented epithelium (CHRPE) is

bilateral and multifocal in FAP

7. APC gene mutation
    - Colectomy only choice
    - 20% have inconclusive APC gene
    - In 25% de novo mutation occurs with no affected ancestors
    - Siblings and children need to be offered genetic testing
    - If inconclusive, offer colonoscopy

8. MAP (MUTYH associated polyposis) is Autosomal recessive
    - Needs two carrier parents
    - Increased risk of gastric and duodenal polyps (and cancer) and should have EGD with a side viewing scope
    - Oligopolyposis
    - Carriers do not have increased risk of warrant increased surveillance

9. Microsatellite instability (MSI) check for patients with CRC < 50 years of age
    - CRC in patients with HNPCC - Tumor tissue positive for MSI

10. Juvenile polyposis syndrome
    - Autosomal dominant
    - Increased CRC and *GASTRIC cancer*, duodenum and pancreas
    - SMAD4, PTEN, BMPR1a mutation and ENG associated with transforming growth factor Beta pathway
    - Patients with SMAD4 pathogenic variants should be evaluated for HHT including screening for and management of cerebral and pulmonary AVMs.

11. Juvenile polyps show mucus filled glands, inflammatory cells, Prominent lamina propria
    - Sporadic juvenile polyps have no increased CRC risk (1-2%)
    - Usually > 5 polyps; > 10 juvenile polyps are rare
    - CRC in 20% with median age of 37
    - Colonoscopy and EGD surveillance at age 12-15 years
        - EGD colonoscopy q1-3 years based on polyp burden
    - Colonoscopy recommended from age 15-70 years
    - Discontinued at 40 years for relatives of patients without confirmed gene mutation

12. Genetic evaluation for any individual with (AGA 2022)
    - 5 or more juvenile polyps of the colon or rectum
    - 2 or more juvenile polyps in other parts of the GI tract
    - Any number of juvenile polyps and first-degree relatives with juvenile polyposis syndrome.

14. Cowden syndrome
    - PTEN mutation
    - **Esophageal acanthosis**
    - Gastric hamartomas
    - Family history of cancer of thyroid and breast
    - Screen for cancers of colon, stomach, small bowel, thyroid, uterus, breast, kidney and melanomas (skin)
    - Colonoscopy surveillance at age 35 years, repeated at intervals no greater than 5 years, depending on polyp burden

15. Cronkhite-Canada syndrome
    - Non-familial
    - Hamartomatous polyps
    - Malabsorption
    - Skin pigmentations
    - Alopecia
    - Nail dystrophy
    - Increased risk of gastric Ca and CRC

16. Serrated polyposis syndrome has BRAF mutations, KRAS and RNF43 gene
    - No germline mutation
    - BRAF and KRAS mutations are mutually exclusive
    - BRAF associated with hypermethylation of MLH1 component
    - This leads to non-inherited silencing of MLH1 promoter
    - Serrated polyposis syndrome needs colonoscopy every year

17. Cold EMR of large serrated polyps with cold snares of smaller lesions
    - Traditional serrated adenomas on left side
    - Seen in 8% of colonoscopies
    - 5% have FDR with serrated polyposis syndrome. Testing of relatives doesn't help
    - Serrated adenomas increase risk of synchronous adenoma
    - 5 serrated polyps proximal to rectum > 5 mm with two > 10 mm
    Or > 20 serrated lesion through out bowel of any size
    - On histology, serrated crypts with branching of crypt bases

18. Hereditary nonpolyposis colon cancer (HNPCC/ Lynch)
    - Colonoscopy at age 20-25
    - Q1-2 years follow up
    - MSH2 or MLH1 gene
    - PMS2 mutation in Lynch is associated with lower risk of colon and endometrial cancer
    - Prophylactic hysterectomy and salpingooophorectomy after childbearing age. Women with Lynch syndrome need to be screened for

endometrial cancer starting age 30
- Aspirin 600 mg reduces the risk of colon cancer but not recommended outside of studies
- Other cancers common in lynch are ovarian, kidney, ureter, bladder, small bowel, stomach, glioblastoma

19. Muir Torre syndrome is a variant of HNPCC with sebaceous adenoma or carcinoma

20. Mismatch repair gene testing is conducted only on cancer and not the polyp

21. Genetic evaluation in Hamartomatous Polyps if (AGA 2022)
    - 2 or more lifetime hamartomatous polyps
    - a family history of hamartomatous polyps
    - Cancer associated with hamartomatous polyposis syndrome in first or second-degree relatives
    - 2 or more histologically confirmed Peutz-Jeghers polyps
    - Any number of Peutz-Jeghers polyps if first-degree relative has Peutz-Jeghers syndrome
    - Characteristic mucocutaneous pigmentation with a family history of Peutz-Jeghers syndrome
    - Any number of Peutz-Jeghers polyps with the characteristic mucocutaneous pigmentation of Peutz-Jeghers syndrome.

21. Peutz-Jeghers syndrome (PJS) are at increased risk for cancer in
    - Breast
    - Small bowel
    - Colon
    - Stomach
    - Pancreas
    - Ovaries
    - Testes
    - Lungs.

22. In PJS (STK11 gene mutation) , baseline video capsule endoscopy or magnetic resonance enterography ages 8-10 years or earlier if the patient is symptomatic
    - If negative, surveillance should resume at age 18.
    - Small bowel surveillance q2-3 years due to risk of small bowel intussusception
    - Polypectomy of small bowel polyps ≥10 mm or symptomatic

23. Baseline EGD and colonoscopy at age 8 -10 year in PJS

- If polyps are detected, both colonoscopy and EGD should be repeated every 2-3 years.
- If no polyps then surveillance at age 18 years, and q3 years

24. PJS- *Annual* pancreatic cancer surveillance with MRI or EUS starting at age 35 years.

25. Hamartomatous polyps seen in
   - PJS
   - Juvenile polyposis syndrome
   - Cowden's

26. Multiple gastrointestinal hamartomas or ganglioneuromas check for Cowden's syndrome and related conditions.

Diverticular Disease and Colitis

1. Diverticulitis has 2 X the risk of colon cancer as general population
   - Avoid NSAIDS
   - Men more likely to have urinary fistula than women due to female organs protecting the urinary bladder
   - Repeat colon after diverticulitis due to increased risk of neoplasm
   - Obesity and age < 50 years associated with recurrent attacks
   - Free perforation after first attack
   - Recurrent attacks in 10-35%
   - Abscess < 4 cm treat with antibiotics
   - Selective use of antibiotics (not IV) in uncomplicated diverticulitis
   - Advise patients with diverticular disease to consider vigorous physical activity. (AGA 2015)

2. Intranuclear viral inclusion in endothelial cells in CMV

3. LUQ pain after a colonoscopy, please consider splenic laceration specially with a drop in Hemoglobin/ BP
   - Treat with IR embolization if stable

4. Segmental colitis associated with diverticular disease (SCADD)
   - Older males
   - Infiltration by neutrophils and lymphocytes, cryptitis and crypt abscesses and architectural distortion
   - Abdominal pain, diarrhea and bleeding
   - No granulation and localization to inter diverticular mucosa with rectum spared
   - Short course of antibiotics or salicylates, rarely steroids/ surgery

5. Microscopic colitis
   - Right colon > left colon- 10% missed by flexible sigmoidoscopy
   - Collagenous colitis associated with NSAIDS affecting middle aged to elderly females
   - Increased risk of celiac disease
   - Increased bile acid seen in the colon and Cholestyramine can be helpful
   - Treatment with budesonide over no treatment for the induction of clinical remission. (AGA 2016)
   - If budesonide therapy is not feasible, then mesalamine, bismuth salicylate, prednisolone (or prednisone)
   - No combination therapy with cholestyramine and mesalamine
   - Recurrence of symptoms after induction therapy, budesonide for maintenance of clinical remission.

6. Collagenous colitis associated with
   - NSAIDS
   - SSRIs
   - Lansoprazole
   - Celiac disease, thyroid disease, rheumatoid arthritis, Type 1 diabetes

7. Young female on OCP or HRT with ischemic colitis likely has factor 5 Leiden issue
   - Factor 5 Leiden assay
   - Commonest genetic abnormality in colonic ischemia is Factor V Leiden, 5% of whites
   - Antiphospholipid antibody is associated with increase in colonic ischemia
   - Ischemic colitis in watershed area - check for factor V Leiden assay

8. Hypotension or systemic low flow state colonic ischemia affects the right colon
   - Local non-occlusive ischemia affects splenic flexure and rectosigmoid
   - Ligation of Inferior mesenteric artery (IMA) affects sigmoid colon
   - Atheromatous emboli short segments of ischemia
   - Systemic low flow states- long segments of ischemia

9. Immune mediated colitis
   - Immune checkpoint inhibitors (ICI) target 3 pathways CTLA4, PD1, PD-L1
   - Occurs 6 weeks after initial dose
   - Activates global T cell response
   - Nivolumab and ipilimumab used in metastatic cancer
   - 5 grades of diarrhea
      1. Mild < 4 (symptomatic Rx, do not DC ICI)
      2. Moderate is 4-6 (PO or IV steroids, CTLA4 held indefinitely, PD1 and PDL1 can be resumed after recovery; Treat with mesalamine or Budesonide)
      3. Severe is >7 BM with fever/ pain (if no response to IV steroids within 2-3 days consider Infliximab; if no response then vedolizumab)
      4. Critical is perforation/ necrosis/ toxic megacolon/ bleeding (Hold all ICI permanently- if no response to IV steroids within 2-3 days consider Infliximab; if no response then vedolizumab)
      5. Death
   - Obtain biopsy of ileum and colon, stomach and duodenum
   - Apoptotic colopathy pattern on biopsy

10. Isolated right colonic ischemia may indicate SMA compromise. Request imaging study of mesenteric vasculature (CTA or MRA ASAP)
    - Isolated right side has worse outcome and greater 30-day mortality
    - More presentation with abdominal pain
    - Less hematochezia
    - Bleeding less common but tends to be more severe
    - Associated with CKD, CAD and Atrial fibrillation
    - Treatment is supportive care, need surgery more often
    - Other causes of colonic ischemia in other areas do not need any further work up as they often resolve spontaneously
    - Associated with A fib, CAD, chronic kidney disease

11. Bone marrow transplantation and typhlitis
    - No colonoscopy
    - Typhlitis is neutropenic enterocolitis
    - Stop chemotherapy
    - IV hydration
    - Broad spectrum antibiotics
    - Bowel rest
    - Surgery for perforation and bleeding sepsis or abscess

12. Solitary rectal ulcer syndrome
    - Median age is around 50 years
    - Anterior wall within 10 cm
    - Need not be solitary
    - Fibrosis in lamina propria with thickening of muscularis mucosal folds
    - Fibromuscular obliteration of lamina propria
    - Rectopexy can be performed

13. Pneumatosis coli
    - Usually spontaneous resolution. Rarely bleeding, pneumoperitoneum, volvulus and obstruction
    - Do not biopsy
    - Associated with lung disease, medications, ischemia, infections or idiopathic
    - Usually asymptomatic and no treatment in asymptomatic patients
    - Increase O2 and Metronidazole to replace hydrogen if symptomatic

14. Radiation proctitis
    - Rectal biopsy may cause fistula, so avoid/ use judiciously
    - Neovascularization is seen in radiation damage
    - Treatment is enemas, oral agents, hyperbaric oxygen, topical agents (NO Formalin that can cause strictures)
    - Endoscopic therapy such as APC (discrete and pulsed), bicap, heater

probe, RFA
- Cryotherapy, 5ASA and corticosteroids not helpful
- Short chain fatty acids helpful in acute radiation proctitis
- Sucralfate enemas may be helpful as initial therapy

15. Tuberculosis (TB) of the IC valve- immigrant from third world country with destroyed IC valve and ulcers
- Colonic biopsies sent of culture and PCR for TB
- Granulomas in submucosa (in Crohn's disease it is granulomas in the mucosa)

16. Use of triptans for migraines associated with ischemic colitis

17. Rectal varices managed by banding or cyanoacrylate glue injection or TIPS

18. GVHD colitis
- Chronic after 100 days of allogeneic stem cell transplant
- GI tract, skin, liver involved
- Apoptotic cells on biopsy
- Treated by steroids to suppress T cell mediated immunity

20. Lower GI Bleed
- Risk stratification score (eg. Oakland</=8) to identify low risk patients for discharge home
- In hemodynamically stable patients, transfusion threshold is 7 gm/dl
- If hemodynamically unstable, consider EGD to rule out upper GI bleed
- Hemostasis can be attempted if INR is < 2.5

21. Reversal of INR in lower GI bleed if hemodynamically unstable or INR levels is excessively high
- Reversal in Afib patients with 4 factor PCC rather than FFP
- Patient patients on DAOC, reversal in life threatening LGIB if no response to resuscitation and cessation
- Targeted reversal agent if DAOC was taken within 24 hours
- No role for anti-fibrinolytic agents such as tranexamic acid in LGIB

22. Platelet transfusion in severe LGIB if < 30 k or < 50 k for endoscopic intervention

23. Colonoscopy recommended to detect bleed
- Non-emergent colonoscopy
- TI intubation if colon source not found
- Clear cap recommended

- Unprepped evaluation or routine flex sig not recommended unless suspected source is distal rectum/ anal canal

24. No colonoscopy if LGI bleeding has subsided and high quality colon has been done within 12 months showing diverticular disease and ruled out CRC
    - Hemodynamically stable recurrent diverticular bleed with recent colonoscopy can be managed conservatively
    - Recurrent bleed after therapy, consider repeating colonoscopy if feasible

25. CT angiogram in patient with hemodynamically significant hematochezia
    - If CTA positive then IR referral for embolization vs colonoscopy in specialized centers
    - Treatment of diverticular bleed with clips, bands or coagulation

26. Discontinue non-aspirin NSAIDS after diverticular hemorrhage
    - Discontinue aspirin for primary cardiovascular prophylaxis
    - Resume aspirin after hospitalization for secondary cardiovascular prophylaxis
    - Aspirin to be continued during hospitalization if possible
    - Providers to evaluate the risk benefit ratio of non-aspirin platelet inhibitors
27. Resume anticoagulation after cessation of LGIB to reduce mortality and thromboembolism

28. Pain is not a part of diverticular bleed and if present consider alternate diagnosis such as colonic ischemia

29. Diverticular bleed
    - Thermal therapy should be avoided in the base of diverticulum due to risk of perforation
    - Epinephrine and hemoclips can be used to manage bleeding in the base
    - Hemoclips are not as effective when placed at the neck of a bleeding diverticulum
    - Endoscopic treatment reduces length of stays, reduces rebleeding rates, surgery rates and embolization rate

30. Diverticular bleed is arterial

31. Acute hemorrhagic rectal ulcer
    - In ICU patients with severe comorbidities
    - Discrete or circumferential and can present with GI hemorrhage
    - Rebleed rate is 25% despite endotherapy

IBS

1. Bristol stool scale for stool form
    - 1-2 constipated
    - 3-4 easy to pass without diarrhea
    - 5,6,7 is mainly diarrhea

2. Motility in small bowel
    - Fed and fasting pattern
    - Fed pattern shows non-propagated focal contractions simultaneously at multiple areas, lasts 4-6 hours after meal
    - Fasting pattern MMC (migratory motor complexes) q 90-120 minutes. Housekeeping propelling undigested foods distally
    - Mediated by cholinergic neurons

3. Mouth to cecum transit time is 6-36 hours. Transit time through right, left and sigmoid colon are 12 hours each

4. IBS-D
    - Use either fecal calprotectin or fecal lactoferrin to screen for IBD
    - Do not use erythrocyte sedimentation rate (ESR) or C-reactive protein (CRP) to screen for IBD. Conflicts with ACG 2021 guidelines to use CRP to r/o IBD along with fecal calprotectin
    - In patients with no RECENT travel history to or recent immigration from high-risk areas, do NOT check for ova and parasites (other than Giardia)
    - Test for celiac disease
    - Test for bile acid diarrhea.
    - Empiric trial of a bile acid binder not recommended per ACG 2021 guidelines
    - No recommendation for the use of currently available serologic tests for diagnosis of IBS.
    - No need for routine colonoscopy, food allergy/sensitivity or stool pathogens in patients < 45y (ACG 2021)
    - No role for probiotics or FMT (ACG 2021)

5. IBS
    - No increase in intestinal or colonic gas
    - No SIBO or colonic methane bacteria in IBS
    - IBS-D if fecal calprotectin elevated then colonoscopy with random biopsies to rule out IBD
    - Lactulose breath test in IBS - first rise in breath H2 is not proven

- IBS-D rule out celiac disease via serology

6. Constipation has increased methanogenic bacteria
   - Methane is increased in constipation

7. Post infectious IBS with negative work up
   - Anxiety/ Depression
   - Use of antibiotics
   - Prolonged disease- highest relative risk
   - Smoking
   - Female sex
   - Toxicity of infecting strain of bacteria
   - Age < 60 years

8. Artificial sweeteners cause osmotic diarrhea
   - Secretory diarrhea is low anion gap diarrhea
   - Osmotic diarrhea is high anion gap diarrhea

9. Stool osmolality < 250 indicates factitious diarrhea
   - Osmotic diarrhea is stool osmolality [2 x (Na+ K)]> 100
   - Secretory diarrhea has osmotic gap < 50
   - Fecal osmolality > 400- stool contamination with concentrated urine or bacterial fermentation

10. Diarrhea with fasting is secretory
    - Large volume diarrhea indicates small bowel source

11. Bile acid malabsorption (BAM) responsible for 30% of IBS-D

12. Four types of BAM
    - Type 1 is ileal disease (surgery, radiation, inflammation)- Rx by cholestyramine
    - Type 2 idiopathic in IBS-D- reduced production of fibroblast growth factor 19 by ileal enterocytes leading to increased hepatic bile acid synthesis
    - Type 3 malabsorption due to SIBO, chronic pancreatitis, post cholecystectomy/ vagotomy, celiac disease
    - Type 4- increased bile synthesis caused by metformin

13. Tests to detect BAM are
    - 75-selenium homotaurocholic acid nuclear medicine scan
    - Total 48 hour stool bile acid measurement
    - Serum fibroblast growth factor 19 level

14. Testing for IBS
    - Check for CRP, CBC
    - Check for Celiac disease (IgA and sTTG) in IBS-D
    - Fecal calprotectin and fecal lactoferrin (Lower quality of data)

15. Rifaximin has a strong recommendation for treating IBS-D
    - Secretagogues such as Plecanatide and linaclotide (Guanylate cyclase activator and CFTR gene) for IBS-C
    - Tegaserod (Zelnorm) for IBS-C for women < 65 years and </= 1 CVS risk factor
    - Tricyclics recommended for pain
    - IBS-D with side effects of imipramine, start Desipramine
    - Eluxadoline also used for IBS-D *contraindicated in pancreatobiliary history including cholecystectomy*
    - Lubiprostone increases chloride channel dependent intestinal fluid secretion
    - Smooth muscle antispasmodic NOT recommended
    - Probiotics NOT recommended for IBS
    - Bile acid sequestrants NOT recommended

16. IBS-D and depression
    - SSRI's cause diarrhea except for Paroxetine that doesn't cause diarrhea. Not recommended for IBS
    - Amitriptyline at low dose would not cause diarrhea

17. Daily Bisacodyl for IBS-C, change to every OTHER day dosing
    - Use soluble fiber instead of insoluble fiber (ACG 2021)
    - Chronic constipation in middle aged person, use Bisacodyl every other day
    - Polyethylene glycol (PEG) recommended (ACG 2021)
    - Patient with IBS-C not responsive to Linaclotide (Linzess), use Lubiprostone (Amitiza) since the mechanism of action is different

18. IBS-C, AGA suggests using
    - Tenapanor
    - Plecanatide
    - Linaclotide
    - Tegaserod for women under the age of 65 years without a history of cardiovascular ischemic events
    - Lubiprostone
    - Polyethylene glycol (PEG) laxatives

19. Cost effective treatment of IBS is low-FODMAP diet
    - The low-FODMAP diet for IBS has 3 phases

- 1) Restriction (lasting no more than 4-6 weeks)
- 2) Reintroduction of FODMAP foods
- 3) Personalization based on results from reintroduction
- If IBS responds to low-FODMAP diet refer to GI dietician to help patient slowly reintroduce foods and detect specific food sensitivities

20. Citalopram may worsen diarrhea
    - Mediterranean diet may worsen bloating
    - Healthy eating advice by the NIH and Care Excellence Guidelines offers benefit to a subset of patients with IBS
    - Gluten free diet in IBS has mixed results on Randomized trials
    - No routine use of biomarkers to predict response to diet

21. Poor candidates for restrictive diet interventions include
    - Consuming few culprit foods
    - Risk for malnutrition
    - Food insecure
    - Eating disorder or uncontrolled psychiatric disorder

22. In patients with IBS, AGA 2022 suggests using
    - Tricyclic antidepressant (TCAs)
    - Antispasmodics
    - No selective serotonin reuptake inhibitors (SSRIs).

23. Kiwi fruits cause least amounts of bloating
    - Prunes have sorbitol that causes bloating. Prunes have acrylamide which is a carcinogen

24. Constipated patient not tolerating fiber with negative colonoscopy, start more aggressive treatment
    - Stop Verapamil if patient constipated
    - In the absence of other symptoms only CBC blood test is needed
    - No colonoscopy for constipation unless for red flags (blood in stools, anemia, weight loss) and age appropriate
    - Laxatives, Lubiprostone and linaclotide (over no drug treatment) in patients with IBS-C. (AGA 2014)

25. IBS-C not responding to low-FODMAP diet or Linoclotide (Linzess) or PEG and negative colonoscopy
    - Treat with Amitiza that works on chloride receptors
    - Plecanatide has action just like Linoclotide (Linzess)
    - Tegaserod only in women < 65 years of age
        - 5-HT4 partial agonist. Contraindicated in patients with cardiovascular history

26. Rifaximin for IBS has only 10% improvement over placebo.
    - Rifaximin not approved IBS-C; only in IBS-D

27. Lubiprostone (Amitiza) works on chloride channel activator increases luminal chloride secretion

28. Linaclotide and Plecanatide are GC-C agonist and increase HCO3- and Cl- secretion via cystic fibrosis transmembrane conductance regulator (CFTR)

29. Tenapanor- GI Na+/ H+ exchanger 3 inhibitor and increases excretion of Na+ and water in stools. Used to treat IBS-C

30. IBS-D
    - Rifaximin, Loperamide, Tricyclics
    - Alosetron (Lotronex) is a serotonin 3 antagonist for treating IBS-D
        - Non-dose dependent ischemic colitis
    - Serology to rule out celiac disease
    - AGA 2022 suggests using eluxadoline, rifaximin, alosetron, loperamide, tricyclic antidepressants (TCAs), antispasmodics
    - If initial response to rifaximin and now with recurrent symptoms, retreat with rifaximin.
    - Do not use selective serotonin reuptake inhibitors (SSRIs).

31. Antispasmodics for IBS
    - No SSRI
    - Not recommended per ACG 2021 guidelines
    - Peppermint can be used (ACG 2021)

32. Eluxadoline is a mu and k-opioid receptor agonist and antagonist of delta opioid receptor for IBS-D
    - Associated risk of pancreatitis
    - Contraindicated in GB surgery, known CBD obstruction, SOD, Alcohol > 3 drinks per day, history of pancreatitis and structural diseases of the pancreas
    - Gallstones not a contraindication

33. Prucalopride is a serotonin 4 agonist for chronic constipation but not IBS-C

34. Cognitive behavioral therapy helps with IBS associated with situation anxiety

35. IBS-D not tolerating Imipramine, but it was effective, switch to Nortriptyline

36. Treatment of constipation in young individual without any red flag symptoms is OTC laxatives

37. Management of opioid induced constipation (OIC) (AGA 2018)
   - In patients with OIC, the AGA recommends use of laxatives as first-line agents
   - Naloxegol (Pamora), Naldemedine, Methylnaltrexone (Relistor) are peripherally activating mu receptor antagonist
   - No Lubiprostone or Prucalopride
   - Alvimopan shortens postoperative ileus

38. Ogelvie's syndrome is acute colonic pseudoobstruction without underlying mechanical obstruction
   - First steps are NG tube decompression, rectal tube with decompression, stop offending agents, correct electrolytes
   - Risk of perforation if cecum is > 12 cm or duration > 6 days
   - If not responsive then endoscopic decompression vs neostigmine
   - Colonoscopy >> Neostigmine 2-5 mg IV (neostigmine first according to ACG)
   - Continuous monitoring of cardiac rhythm and respiratory status and immediate access to atropine (antidote to neostigmine) in the event of bradycardia
   - Glycopyrrolate may be useful in preventing side effects of the medication

39. Serum Trypsin/ Trypsinogen indicates pancreatic insufficiency
   - H2 breath test indicates bacterial overgrowth
   - Celiac panel indicates celiac disease

40. Sigmoid volvulus- Convex towards patient's right. Treat by sigmoidoscopy
   - Cecal volvulus is convex to patient's left- surgical management. Do not attempt colonoscopy due to risk of perforation

41. IBS-D with depression, treatment with paroxetine (no side effects of diarrhea) others may cause diarrhea

42. Carnett's sign
   - Localized tenderness that is worse with tensing abdominal muscles usually in T7-12 distribution due to a sensory nerve irritation

43. IBS with bloating- treat SIBO with rifaximin

44. E Coli affecting small bowel
    - Enterotoxigenic EC- Traveler's diarrhea
    - Enteropathogenic EC - Diarrhea in children (Pediatric)
    - Enteroadherent E Coli cause diarrhea in AIDS (and children)

45. E Coli affecting colon
    - Enteroinvasive EC and Enterohemorrhagic E coli- Shiga Toxin
    - Severe diarrhea O157:H7, hemolytic uremic syndrome
    - Avoid antibiotics and antidiarrheals

46. Chronic idiopathic constipation
    - Use fiber over no fiber. Psyllium husk has the best evidence
    - PEG over no PEG
    - MgO over no MgO
        - Avoid in renal patient due to risks of hypermagnesemia
    - Those who fail OTC therapy use lactulose or Lubiprostone (with food),
    Linaclotide, Plecanatide, Prucalopride
    - Short term bisacodyl or sodium picosulfate over no sodium picosulfate
    - Senna over no Senna

47. Senna or anthraquinone laxatives cause melanosis coli

48. Centrally mediated abdominal pain syndrome
    - Central sensitization with disinhibition of pain signals
    - More in women in 4th decade of life
    - Unrelated to food or bowel habits

49. Fecal impaction may not always be detected on digital rectal examination
in a patient with overflow diarrhea. Check with abdominal x-ray

Infections

1. E Coli affecting colon
   - Enteroinvasive E coli and Enterohemorrhagic E coli- Shiga Toxin
   - Severe diarrhea O157:H7, hemolytic uremic syndrome
   - Avoid antibiotics and antidiarrheals
   - Supportive care only

2. Homosexual man with rectal ulcer
   - HSV
   - Chlamydia trachomatis (Diagnosed by nucleic acid amplification test)
   - Treponema pallidum (Syphillis)
     - Rectal syphilis is treated by Benzathine penicillin 2.4 million units

3. Stool cultures prior to treatment
   - Bloody diarrhea in the US
   - Watery diarrhea with fever or > 3 days in duration
   - Not in travelers of high-risk areas. Treat instead with azithromycin

4. Patient with recurrence of C diff infection (CDI) after Metronidazole.
   - Treat with vancomycin 125 mg QID PO x 10 days
   - If recurrence after vancomycin, then 10-day course of fidaxomicin

5. Non- severe C diff infection (CDI)
   - Vancomycin 125 mg 4 times a day x 10 days first line of treatment
     - Safe in pregnancy and breastfeeding
   - Fidaxomicin 200 mg twice daily for 10 days
   - Vancomycin or fidaxomicin can be used first line for treatment of CDI in patients who are immunocompromised.
   - Metronidazole 500 mg 3 times daily for 10 days
   - Use probiotics only in the context of a clinical trial
   - Improvement but mild symptoms after C diff infection is probably post infectious IBS that occurs in 25%
     - Treated with Imodium
     - PCR can be positive for 1 month after C diff infection. Doesn't check for Toxin A or B

6. Severe CDI
   - White blood cell (WBC) ≥15,000 cells/mm3
   - Serum creatinine >1.5 mg/dL.
   - Initial therapy for severe CDI
     - Vancomycin 125 mg 4 times a day for 10 days
     - Fidaxomicin 200 mg twice daily or 10 days

7. Fulminant C diff infection
   - Patients meeting criteria for severe C. difficile infection and
   - Hypotension or shock or ileus or megacolon

8. Treatment of fulminant CDI (ACG 2021)
   - Adequate volume resuscitation
   - 500 mg of oral vancomycin every 6 hours daily
   - Parenteral metronidazole 500 mg every 8 hours
   - In ileus, the addition of vancomycin enemas (500 mg every 6 hours) may be beneficial

9. Fulminant C diff who require surgical intervention
   - Total colectomy with an end ileostomy and a stapled rectal stump or
   - A diverting loop ileostomy with colonic lavage and intraluminal vancomycin
   - Fecal microbiota transplant (FMT) is considered for patients with severe and fulminant CDI refractory to antibiotic therapy when patients are deemed poor surgical candidates

10. Recurrent CDI (ACG 2021)
    - Tapering/pulsed-dose vancomycin for patients with first recurrence after an initial course of fidaxomicin, vancomycin, or metronidazole
    - Fidaxomicin for patients experiencing a first recurrence after an initial course of vancomycin or metronidazole
    - FMT for patients experiencing their second or further recurrence of CDI
       - FMT delivered through colonoscopy or capsules
       - Enema if other methods are unavailable
       - Repeat FMT for patients experiencing a recurrence of CDI within 8 weeks of an initial FMT
       - Not for first recurrence

11. Vancomycin 125 mg p.o. 4 times a day for a minimum of 14 days in patients with IBD and CDI

12. Prevention of CDI (ACG 2021)
    - For patients with recurrent CDI who are not candidates for FMT, who relapsed after FMT, or who require ongoing or frequent courses of antibiotics, long-term suppressive oral vancomycin may be used to prevent further recurrences
    - Oral vancomycin prophylaxis
    - Bezlotoxumab used for prevention of *CDI recurrence* in patients who are at high risk of recurrence, *usually after 3rd recurrence*
    - No need to stop PPI to reduce CDI

13. In adults and children on antibiotic treatment for prevention of C difficile infection (AGA)
- S boulardii alone or
- The 2-strain combination of L acidophilus CL1285 and L casei LBC80R
- The 3-strain combination of L acidophilus, L delbrueckii subsp bulgaricus, and B bifidum
- The 4-strain combination of L acidophilus, L delbrueckii subsp bulgaricus, B bifidum, and S salivarius subsp thermophilus
- Use of probiotics in IBS, UC or CD only in context of a clinical trial
- No Probiotics for prevention of C diff infection (ACG 2021)

14. Entamoeba histolytica is associated with travel and is treated with 7-day course of Metronidazole followed by paromomycin, diloxanide, iodoquinol

15. Antidiarrheals such as loperamide avoided in patients with dysentery

16. Multiplex PCR testing doesn't indicate viable organisms. Culture detects viable organisms

17. Traveler's diarrhea prophylaxis with Bismuth subsalicylate 2 tabs x 4 times daily
- Traveller's diarrhea in South Asia treated with Azithromycin 1 gm once due to presence of fluoroquinolone resistant campylobacter

5. IBD

IBD Introduction

1. IBD has a bimodal peak between 15 -30 years and then 50-80 years
   - More common in jewish population and less common in hispanics and blacks

2. In ulcerative colitis (UC) the inflammation is localized to mucosal layer
   - Rectum is involved
   - Involves colon in a continuous manner
   - Appendiceal patch is diagnostic of UC (even with patchy skip area) and not CD

3. Crohn's disease (CD) has transmural inflammation with skip areas of involvement
   - Associated with strictures, fistulas, fibrosis
   - Involves commonly TI and proximal colon but can affect any part of GI tract

4. Smoking and lack of physical activity are risk factors for Crohn's but not for UC
   - Increased smoking associated with worse disease

5. There is an association between IBD and isotretinoin used in treatment of acne

6. Pathogenesis of IBD appears to be a failure of the innate mucosal immune system

7. Nod2 gene located on chromosome 16 plays a key role in bacterial recognition and binding. Mutations are noted in many patients with Crohn's disease

8. IBD is associated with Turner's syndrome

9. Non-caseating granulomas on biopsy is consistent with Crohn's
10. Increased risk of squamous cell cancer of the anus and vulva with CD
    - Lactose intolerance common
    - Women are at higher risk

11. Crohn's CDAI index - Abdominal pain is included in the score

12. Severe UC vs mild UC - Hb < 75% of normal

13. Truelove Witts criteria of severe UC
    - > 6 BM per day
    - Temp> 37.8
    - Hb< 10.5
    - ESR> 30
    - HR> 90

14. Moderate to severe UC had up to 10 bowel movements daily, ESR > 30 and elevated CRP
    - Fulminant UC > 10 bowel movements per day or transfusion requirement

15. p-ANCA in UC
    - Occurs in ⅔ of UC and ¼ of CD- usually Crohn's colitis
    - ASCA IgG increased with CD
    - p-ANCA not associated with disease activity
    - Doesn't decrease by colectomy
    - Increased risk of pouchitis after colectomy if titers of p-ANCA are high

16. Telemedicine is not better than in person IBD visit

17. In IBD patients with strictures, recommend low residue diet otherwise no specific dietary restrictions

18. Immune check point inhibitors mimic IBD
    - for more than mild symptoms, treat with steroids and if unresponsive then infliximab

Extraintestinal manifestations

1. Extraintestinal manifestations that are independent of disease activity in IBD
   - HLA B27 associated with central axial arthritis (Ankylosing spondylitis, Sacroiliitis) and Uveitis
   - First line therapy for ankylosing spondylitis is physical therapy
   - PSC, Pyoderma gangrenosum, sacroiliitis, Uveitis, Iritis and ankylosing spondylitis doesn't parallel disease activity.
   - X-ray of bamboo spine consistent with ankylosing spondylitis is suggestive of IBD

2. Extraintestinal manifestation that parallels disease activity in IBD
   - Erythema nodosum, Aphthous ulcers, Episcleritis, Scleritis, peripheral arthritis, Sweet syndrome (acute febrile neutrophilic dermatosis) parallel disease activity
   - Peripheral arthritis affects large joints
       - Asymmetrical
   - No HLA B27

3. IBD with highest rate of fracture
   - Steroids > 3 months
   - IBD with prior fracture
   - Post-menopausal females

4. IBD and osteoporosis
   - 17-41% shows osteoporosis
   - 22-77% show osteopenia
   - Mild increase in fracture over general population
   - Most frequent site is the spine
   - Active IBD disease with reduced bone mineral density in both sexes
   - Bisphosphonates (not vitamin D or calcium) reduce the risk of fractures

5. Pyoderma gangrenosum
   - 20-50% Of IBD
   - Pathergy (worsened with trauma)
   - Independent of disease activity
   - Peristomal pyoderma gangrenosum more common in women and can occur years after an ostomy
   - Treatment is local steroids, infliximab (or Anti-TNF), Azathioprine, Dapsone, topical Tacrolimus and cyclosporine

6. Hidradenitis suppurativa

- Increased with IBD
- First line therapy is oral antibiotics (tetracycline or Clinda + Rifampin)
- Second line is Infliximab, Adalimumab (Not Etanercept), antiandrogens, metformin, retinoids

7. In hospitalized patients with acute severe UC, DVT prophylaxis recommended to prevent venous thromboembolism

8. Primary sclerosing cholangitis (PSC) occurs in 7.5% of UC and 75% of PSC have UC
   - UC is more likely to be pancolitis, with greater backwash ileitis and rectal sparing
   - Significantly increased risk of colon cancer
      - Colonoscopy q 1-2 years
   - Increased risk of cholangiocarcinoma
   - PSC follows course independent of UC
   - IBD patient with elevated liver enzymes particularly alkaline phosphatase, consider MRCP to r/o PSC

9. Autoimmune hemolytic anemia is an uncommon association with UC pancolitis
   - May parallel disease activity
   - Sulfasalazine may cause hemolytic anemia in patients with G6PD deficiency

10. Crohn's patients with ileal disease are at a risk of oxalate stones
   - Treat by calcium supplementation

IBD and Pregnancy

1. In pregnancy, UC is more likely to flare than CD
   - Events in one pregnancy are unlikely to recur in subsequent pregnancies
   - ⅓ of patients with IBD flares up during pregnancy

2. CD and pregnancy
   - Remission before pregnancy is likely to remain in remission
   - Methotrexate to be discontinued 3 months before planned pregnancy (AGA)
   - Fertility is normal in inactive IBD in the absence of extensive surgery
   - Fertility is lower in women with active disease, Ileal anal pouch anastomosis (IPAA), permanent colostomy or proctectomy due to scarring of fallopian tubes
   - Pregnancy not contraindicated with ileostomy
   - Flares commonest in first trimester and soon after delivery

3. IBD and pregnancy (AGA 2018)
   - Aminosalicylates and thiopurines can be continued throughout
   - Corticosteroids only for flares and not for maintenance
     - Safe for pregnancy
     - Safe for breastfeeding
     - Hypothalamic pituitary adrenal gland axis only depressed after 3 weeks of > 20 mg/ day of prednisone
   - Biologics continued throughout with one dose in last trimester to deliver the baby during the drug trough. Crosses placenta after 20 weeks
   - Avoid live vaccine in the child after biologics in utero *except for certolizumab*
   - Certolizumab doesn't cross the placenta
   - Stool softeners and antibiotics as needed

4. Pregnant IBD patients have increased preterm labor, low birth weight and small for gestational age babies
   - Premature birth unrelated to AZT

5. Vaginal delivery contraindicated for ACTIVE perianal CD or history of previous vaginal fistulas
   - Increased risk with vaginal delivery with inactive perianal CD but could be considered

6. Contraception in women and IBD
   -   Non-estrogen   containing   contraception   due   to   risk   of

thromboembolism
- Low dose estrogen contraceptive in patient with no personal or family history of thromboembolism
- Hormonal or non-hormonal intrauterine device (IUD)
- Contraceptive implant

7. Options for management of flares in IBD during pregnancy
   - Routine IBD labs, CRP and ESR, Fecal calprotectin, drug levels. Objective measures of inflammation improve long term remission rates in IBD
   - Labs elevated in pregnancy CRP and ESR.
   - *Flexible sigmoidoscopy* over pancolonoscopy, unsedated and unprepped in any trimester
   - Gadolinium avoided in pregnancy
   - Single CT scan radiation exposure is below level of concern.
       - MRI and CT have similar diagnostic accuracy
   - Ultrasound for terminal ileal disease
   - Surgery for acute severe colitis, perforation, abscess, severe hemorrhage or bowel obstruction
   - Avoid thiopurines in naive patients for the first time in pregnancy

8. Do not use methotrexate, tofacitinib and s1p receptor agonists during pregnancy or breastfeeding

9. Medications during pregnancy
   - Mesalamine - Maintain pre pregnancy dose
       - Ok for breastfeeding; monitor child for diarrhea
   - Sulfasalazine- consider 2 mg folic acid along with the medication
   - *Azulfidine may have phthalate and contraindicated*
   - OK for breastfeeding, mesalamine preferred

10. Medications during pregnancy:
    - Immunomodulators: dosing change due to increased renal clearance. Drug levels monitored. OK for breastfeeding
    - Biologics continue pre pregnancy dose and *compatible with breastfeeding*
        - Adalimumab stopped 2-3 weeks before delivery
        - Infliximab, Ustekinumab, Vedolizumab 6-10 weeks before expected delivery or 4-5 weeks before expected delivery if given every 4 weeks
    - Resume biologics 48 hours after cesarean delivery if no infection
        - 24 hours after vaginal delivery

11. Medications during pregnancy
    - Corticosteroids reserved for flares during pregnancy, compatible with breastfeeding
        - Avoid feeding 1-2 hours after a dose

- Antibiotics: Augmentin over Cipro for perianal disease. No maintenance therapy, compatible with breastfeeding
- Avoid fenugreek for milk stimulation

IBD Therapy

1. Goals of IBD therapy (STRIDE II)
   - Clinical remission
   - Tissue healing
   - Improvement in functional outcomes
   - Endoscopic healing (not histologic remission) is the target of IBD therapy

2. Management of UC: (AGA 2023)
   - Monitor symptomatic remission with markers and symptoms rather than symptoms alone
      - Fecal calprotectin < 150 and normal CRP

3. UC with mild symptoms and normal markers, need endoscopic evaluation of disease activity
   - Mild symptoms with elevated markers, endoscopic evaluation over treatment adjustment
   - Patients with symptomatic remission but elevated markers, need endoscopic evaluation

4. Moderate to severe symptoms with elevated markers such as CRP, calprotectin and lactoferrin, treatment adjustments over endoscopic evaluation

5. No recommendations for biomarker based monitoring of UC over endoscopy based monitoring

6. Aminosalicylates are the cornerstone of therapy in *mild* to moderate UC
   - No role for 5-ASA in management of of CD

7. IBD therapy for CD and moderate to severe UC
   - Early use of biologic agents with or without immunomodulator rather than gradual step up after failure of 5-ASA

8. All patient being started on anti-TNF need hepatitis B and interferron gamma release assay for TB in addition to routine labs such as CBC, CMP, HFP and inflammatory markers

7. Therapy of moderate to severe UC (AGA 2020)
   - Infliximab, adalimumab, golimumab, vedolizumab, tofacitinib, or ustekinumab over no treatment

8. Therapy of moderate to severe UC and naïve to biologics, *infliximab or vedolizumab rather than adalimumab,* for induction
  - Adalimumab as an alternative for convenience
  - Tofacitinib can be used only after failure or intolerance to TNF-α antagonists.

9. Primary non-response to infliximab in UC
  - Ustekinumab or tofacitinib rather than vedolizumab or adalimumab for induction

10. UC -NO thiopurine monotherapy for induction
  - Thiopurine monotherapy for maintenance of remission.

11. UC in remission
  - *Combination therapy* (TNF-α antagonists, vedolizumab or ustekinumab with thiopurines or methotrexate) *over* biologic or thiopurine *monotherapy*
  - *No role for using biologic monotherapy or tofacitinib over thiopurine monotherapy for maintenance of remission.*

12. Induction of remission in moderate to severe CD
  - Patients naïve to biologics and immunomodulators, *combination therapy* (Infliximab or Adalimumab + thiopurines) *over monotherapy* with biologic for the induction and maintenance of remission

13. Induction of remission in moderate to severe CD
  - Infliximab, adalimumab, or ustekinumab and perhaps vedolizumab (not certolizumab) for the induction of remission (AGA 2021)

14. Induction of remission in moderate to severe CD
  - Nonresponse to anti-TNFα (primary nonresponse or mechanistic failure), *use ustekinumab* (or vedolizumab) for the induction

15. Secondary non response ie. those who previously responded to infliximab in CD, use adalimumab or ustekinumab (or vedolizumab)

16. Use corticosteroids over no treatment for induction of remission in CD
  - No thiopurines alone for achieving remission
  - Budesonide may be used for induction

17. In severe or fuliminant CD, treated with IV steroids

18. Demyelinating condition such as MS is a contraindication to TNF inhibitor.

19. Quiescent moderate to severe CD (or patients in corticosteroid-induced remission), thiopurines over no treatment for the maintenance of remission.

20. Quiescent CD
   - No recommendation for withdrawal of either the immunomodulator or the biologic over ongoing combination therapy
   - Thiopurines over no treatment for the maintenance.
   - No corticosteroids for maintenance

21. CD with fistula
   - No certolizumab pegol
   - Use Infliximab (strong), adalimumab, ustekinumab, or vedolizumab for the induction or maintenance of fistula remission.
   - *Biologic + antibiotic over a biologic or antibiotic alone for the induction of fistula remission.*

22. Perianal abscess needs to be diagnosed, drained and treated prior to starting biologic for fistulizing CD

23. In patients on anti-TNF biologic, reactive therapeutic drug monitoring with drug and antibody level recommended over empiric drug escalation or switching medications

24. IBD and loss of response to biologicals
   - If Infliximab levels therapeutic and no antibodies then use a biological with a different mechanism of action
   - If undetected Infliximab level and positive antibody
      - Do not use biosimilars
      - Use a different TNF antagonist in combination with Azathioprine or Methotrexate

25. Crohn's disease with good response to infliximab
   - Non stricturing disease
   - Colonic disease
   - Short duration
   - Non-smoker

26. Increased risk of antibody formation to infliximab with
   - Low albumin
   - High inflammatory markers
   - HLA-DQA1*05

27. Progressive escalation of biologic dose needed to keep IBD under control

may indicate antibody formation

28. Hospitalized patients use IV methylprednisolone dose equivalent to 40–60 mg/d rather than higher doses of IV corticosteroids

29. In refractory UC pancolitis that failed IV steroid treatment, options are infliximab or cyclosporine
    - Anti-TNF at 0,2 and 6 weeks or cyclosporine 2-4 mg/kg
    - Infliximab and cyclosporine were similar in colectomy rate
    - Infliximab can be continued as maintenance therapy, but cyclosporine needs to be switched to azathioprine
        - *Cyclosporine rescue is therefore not long term*
    - If infliximab or cyclosporine fail in refractory UC, then colectomy

30. Do NOT use cyclosporine rescue after infliximab failure in severe UC pancolitis
    - No role for sequential treatment of cyclosporine and infliximab as it is associated with increased infection and death

32. CMV colitis seen in 30% of steroid refractory colitis and has higher risk of colectomy

33. Hospitalized patient without infection, NO adjunctive antibiotics.

34. Anti-TNF agents associated with palmoplantar pustulosis and psoriasiform lesions on extensor surface
    - Psoriasiform lesions, treat through this or switch to a different anti-TNF agent
    - Pustulosis, change the medication to a different category
        - Ustekinumab for Crohn's disease maybe an alternative

35. Methotrexate used in CD along with TNF inhibitor to prevent Ab development

36. Infliximab (Remicade) associated with melanoma
    - Not associated with solid tumors

37. Natalizumab causes PML because it binds to both alpha4B1 and alpha4B7 and crosses the blood brain barrier.
    - Vedolizumab only binds to alpha4B7 (MADCAM 1)

38. Better response to Vedolizumab if
    - Treatment naive to Anti-TNF
    - Disease duration > 2 years

- Higher albumin
- Moderate disease activity

39. Vedolizumab has a slower onset of action

40. Vedolizumab not associated with solid tumor or lymphoma risk.
    - No change in infection rates between vedolizumab and placebo

41. Crohn's on infliximab with myalgia, arthralgia and fever x 1 week after infusion- likely due to hypersensitivity, treat with steroids

42. Mild to moderate UC
    - Mesalamine tried before budesonide
    - Once daily mesalamine is better than twice daily
    - Higher doses better than lower doses

43. UC with tofacitinib (JAK inhibitor)
    - Zoster (VZ) vaccine
    - Screen for venous thromboembolismcoagulation syndromes due to increased risk of thromboembolism and arterial thrombosis
    - Increased risk of heart failure with Infliximab or tofacitinib
    - Check lipid panel

44. S1P receptor modulators contraindicated in pregnancy
    - Ozanimod is used to treat adults with moderate to severe UC
    - Need to be tested for antibodies against Varicella zoseter virus and vaccinated if negative
    - Blocks the migration of lymphocytes from LN to site of inflammation
    - Cardiovascular events are rare but may cause nasopharyngitis and anemia

45. Mesalamine
    - Can cause hypersensitivity
    - Olsalazine may cause secretory diarrhea
    - Interstitial nephritis, pneumonitis and acute pancreatitis are idiosyncratic
    - Sulfasalazine (and not mesalamine) may cause reduced fertility due to reduced sperm motility and change is reversible

46. In mild to moderate UC (AGA 2018)
    - Extensive mild–moderate UC, standard-dose mesalamine (2–3 g/d) or diazo-bonded 5-ASA rather than low-dose mesalamine, sulfasalazine, or no treatment.
    - Sulfasalazine in patients with prominent arthritic symptoms 2–4 g/d

- Extensive or left-sided mild–moderate UC, add rectal mesalamine to oral 5-ASA.

47. In patients with mild to moderate UC and suboptimal response to standard-dose mesalamine use high-dose mesalamine (>3 g/d) with rectal mesalamine.
- Mesalamine or diazo-bonded 5-ASA, rather than budesonide MMX or controlled ileal release budesonide for induction of remission.
- In patients with left-sided disease, mesalamine enemas (or suppositories) rather than oral mesalamine.
- Mesalamine enemas rather than rectal corticosteroids.

48. If UC refractory to oral and rectal 5-ASA, add either oral prednisone or budesonide MMX.
- No curcumin (Turmeric- RCT has shown improvement), probiotics or FMT

49. Patient with active disease on Azathioprine with low 6 TGN (active metabolite- Leukopenia) and low 6MMPN (liver toxicity)
- Increase the dose of Azathioprine

50. If patient with CD on remission with Azathioprine monotherapy, continue Azathioprine monotherapy

51. Low 6TGN with high 6MMPN while on Azathioprine
- Refractory of 6MP due to too much shunt
- Allopurinol blocks Xanthine Oxidase and prevents metabolism of 6TGN to 6MMPN
- Monitor for leukopenia- check CBC
- Gene NUDT15 associated with leukopenia

52. Pancreatitis from 6MP/ Allopurinol is Idiosyncratic
- 6 MP active metabolite increased with 5 ASA coadministration

53. Thiopurine (AZT/ 6MP) increase the risk of nonmelanoma skin cancer, cervical cancer and lymphoma

54. AZT/ 6 MP and Lymphoma
- Increased risk of lymphoma only after 1 year of treatment
- Patients < 30 years have higher relative risk, but patients > 50 years have the greatest absolute risk
  - Absolute risk higher in patients > 50 years
  - Relative risk of Lymphoma highest in teens
- Only increased with active therapy (Risk only in current users)

- Men at higher risk

55. Three types of Lymphomas associated with AZT
   - 2 related to EBV
      - Post-transplant like Lymphoma
      - Early Post mononuclear Lymphoma
   - Hepatosplenic T cell
      - Anti-TNF + AZT
      - < 32 years of age
      - Risk reduces to baseline after stopping AZT

56. COVID vaccine 2 doses for all > 12 years. 3rd dose for immunosuppressed

57. Probiotics
   - Maintenence therapy of pouchitis
   - 8-strain combination of L paracasei subsp paracasei, L plantarum, L acidophilus, L delbrueckii subsp bulgaricus, B longum subsp longum, B breve, B longum subsp infantis, and S salivarius subsp thermophilus
   - Preventing C diff in patients on antibiotics (only in studies)
   - Preventing necrotizing enterocolitis in preterm babies
   - Use of probiotics in IBS, UC or CD only in context of a clinical trial

58. Non-live vaccine such as Pneumococcal vaccine safe in immunocompromised

59. Steroid dependent CD with joint symptoms
   - Methotrexate at 25 mg weekly sq only in CD (not UC)

60. Patients with IBD need to be screened annually for PSC and side effects of medications

61. If > 1/3rd of colon involved, then surveillance 8-10 years after disease onset

IBD and Surgery

1. High risk of post operative CD recurrence
    - Age< 30 years
    - 2 prior resections
    - Penetrating or fistulizing disease
    - Active smoking
    - Treat with biological + metronidazole 500 mg TID PO x 3 months

2. Low risk of post operative CD recurrence
    - Age > 50 years
    - Disease duration > 10 years
    - Short segment disease (less than 10-20 cm)
    - Stricture < 10 cm
    - First resection/ surgery
    - Fibrostenotic disease
    - Non-smoker
    - Treat with Metronidazole 500 mg TID PO x 3 months

3. Ileocolonoscopy 6-12 months after surgery with endoscopy guided treatment to decrease risk of recurrent CD

4. Less than 5 ulcers is low risk for postop recurrence of CD

5. Rutgeerts score used for post operative assessment of Crohn's disease
    - i0 is no ulcerations
    - i1 < 5 aphthous lesions
    - i2 > 5 aphthous lesions, passable strictures, lesion at anastomosis
    - i3 diffuse ileitis
    - i4 ileitis with ulcerations and stenosis

6. Clinical recurrence of CD after surgery occurs at anastomotic site and in 60% of patients
    - Endoscopic recurrence is higher than clinical recurrence

7. Pouchitis
    - Probiotics maintain remission in pouchitis
    - 50% get pouchitis
    - Development of fistula soon after surgery may indicate anastomotic leak

8. Causes of increased risk of pouchitis
    - Extensive UC
    - Extraintestinal manifestations

- PSC
- Backwash ileitis
- Increased pANCA
- Need for steroids before surgery
- Interleukin-1 receptor antagonist polymorphisms
- NOD2/CARD15

9. NSAIDS cause secondary pouchitis that may not respond to antibiotics

10. Cipro is better than Metronidazole for pouchitis
    - CD needs to be ruled out if symptoms do not improve with Cipro

11. Pouch prolapse presents with pain bleeding and inability to pass stools

12. Ileoanal pouch failure is 1-2% in UC due to pelvic sepsis and pouchitis
    - Pouch failure in Crohn's is 10-15%

13. Adhesions from ileal pouch anal anastomosis may interfere with conceptions in women

14. Cuffitis
    - UC involving the mucosa of the anal cuff after ileal pouch anal anastomosis (IPAA)
    - Presents with bleeding unlike pouchitis

15. Large transverse colon on KUB- toxic megacolon
    - Mortality with perforation is > 40%
    - Mortality without perforation is 10%
    - Treatment is total colectomy

16. In patients with surgically induced remission of CD, early pharmacological prophylaxis over endoscopy-guided pharmacological treatment. (AGA 2017)
    - Anti-TNF therapy and/or thiopurines over other agents
    - No mesalamine, budesonide, or probiotics
    - Postoperative endoscopic monitoring in all patients at 6 to 12 months after surgical resection
    - Asymptomatic endoscopic recurrence, anti-TNF and/or thiopurine therapy over continued monitoring alone

IBD and C Diff

1. IBD refractory to treatment should rule out C diff infection. Can develop without history of antibiotics
    - if IBD flare, r/o C diff

2. UC with C diff infection with severe complicated CDI
    - ICU admission
    - Vancomycin 500 mg PO QID
    - Metronidazole 500 mg IV TID
    - Vanco PR 500 mg QID
    - FMT not indicated due to risk of perforation

3. Crohn's ileocolitis with recurrent C diff - treat with FMT
    - Flares of IBD possible
    - No significant infections with FMT

IBD Potpourri

1. IBD patient on immunosuppressive treatment, annual PAP and HPV can be administered

2. CD is least likely to be misdiagnosed as IBS-D

3. Long history of Crohn's stricture with recent weight loss - likely malignancy, surgery consult

4. Increased fecal calprotectin indicating inflammation is an indicator of recurrence of IBD after de escalation therapy

5. If biopsies show HGD, repeat colonoscopy with chromoendoscopy in 3 months
    - Low grade dysplasia in a resected lesion, repeat colon in 6 months
    - Increased risk of high grade dysplasia with sessile large lesions
    - If dysplasia doesn't respond to EMR then surgery referral

6. Small bowel ulceration causes increased fecal calprotectin

7. Slide with microabscesses is suggestive of UC. Treat with mesalamine

8. CT/ MR enterogram
    - Transmural disease assessment
    - Extraintestinal disease assessment
    - Penetrating disease assessment
    - Alters management plans for up to 50% of patients

9. MRI of the pelvis best test for perianal fistulizing disease
    - CT usefulness limited due to bone artifact
    - Infliximab and azathioprine combo has the best data

10. Amyloidosis due to IBD has deposition of AA amyloid fibrils which are an acute phase reactant

11. COVID and IBD
    - Worse in IBD patients on steroids
    - Is no different in IBD patients on biologics
    - Stop biologicals when patients get COVID

6. LIVER

ACUTE LIVER FAILURE (ALF)

1. In ALF with type 2 or greater encephalopathy, early continuous renal replacement therapy even in the absence of conventional indicators for hyperammonemia

2. No correction of coagulopathy in the absence of bleeding or planned high risk procedure

3. Antimicrobial agents do not improve rate of infection or 21 day mortality in ALF

4. Refractory hypotension norepinephrine first line
    - Vasopressin if norepinephrine not effective

5. Non-APAP ALF, IV NAC recommended

6. HBV associated with ALF, initiate anti-HBV therapy
    - Entecavir or tenofovir based regimen

7. Mushroom poisoning - IV silibinin
    - IV Penicillin G if silibinin unavailable
    - Presents with acute gastroenteritis within 6-12 hours and ALF in 1-2 days
    - Escudie criteria for assessing the need for liver transplantation in ALF and mushroom poisoning
    - Gastric lavage and activated charcoal if early

8. King's college criteria or MELD score used in ALF
    - Poor prognosis if MELD > 25

9. KCC
    - Arterial pH < 7.3, lactate > 3
    - INR > 6.5, Creatinine > 3.4, HE > 3

10. In suspected alcoholic liver disease PETH and ethyl glucuronide used in addition to thorough history

11. Hepatic encephalopathy 2 needs ICU monitoring
    - Encephalopathy 3 or 4 - intubated for airway protection

12. Liver biopsy in ALF
    - Transjugular to r/o AIH and infiltrative disease or malignancy

13. Equivocal evidence for routine ICP monitoring, hypothermia, lactulose, rifaximin

14. INR doesn't predict bleeding risk in ALF
   - *Viscoelastic tests* more accurate

15. Clinical signs of infections are often absent in ALF
   - Empiric antibiotics/ antifungal agents can be considered with clinical deterioration
   - Regular surveillance cultures

16. Continuous renal replacement therapy over intermittent for
   - Kidney injury
   - Electrolyte or metabolic abnormalities
   - Volume overload

17. Enteral nutritional support started if no PO intake in 5-7 days

18. No support for artificial/ bioartificial liver support devices or plasma exchange in ALF

19. Activated charcoal within 4 hours if APAP ingestion

20. IV Acyclovir empirically for ALF and suspected grade 2 HSV encephalitis
   - Confirmatory PCR

21. Wilson's disease with ALF, early liver transplantation
   - Coombs negative hemolytic anemia

22. AIH treated with IV corticosteroids or liver transplantation with ALF

23. Pregnancy related ALF, prompt delivery of fetus
   - If no improvement then liver transplantation
   - Half the causes of ALF in pregnancy are not specific for pregnancy

24. BCS associated ALF, treat with heparin
   - TIPS if anticoagulation not helpful
   - Liver transplantation if above not helpful

25. ALF with 1A priority, Liver donors can be considered as well as ABO-1 grafts in rapidly declining patients

26. ALF is Hyperacute if < 7 days
   - Acute 1-3 weeks
   - Subacute 3 weeks-6 months

27. APAP toxicity
- Marked transaminitis with relatively low T bili
- Rapid progression to ALF with hypoglycemia, renal failure and lactic acidosis within 72-96 hours

28. In ischemic liver injury, T bili and INR worsen despite improving transaminases

29. In acute on chronic liver failure, HE responds to lactulose/ Rifaximin

30. Herpes simplex hepatitis with failure
- Relatively normal or low T bili
- Change in mental status

Pregnancy and Liver disease

1. Most common liver disease during pregnancy is viral hepatitis
   - Young patient with acute hepatitis and jaundice: Discharge for outpatient monitoring

2. Pregnancy increases Alkaline phosphatase (ALP)
   - Decreases GGT, T Bili and Albumin
   - No change in AST and ALT

3. Third trimester with cholestasis of pregnancy with no maternal or fetal distress, treat with URSO
   - GGT is normal
   - T Bili is not elevated
   - Serum bile salts are increased >10
   - Serum bile acid > 40 is associated with worse prognosis.
   - Recurrent rate is 70% in subsequent pregnancies

4. Recurrent 3rd trimester problems in subsequent pregnancies
   - Preeclampsia with HTN, proteinuria and edema
   - Acute fatty liver of pregnancy (AFLP)
   - HELLP is also common in preeclampsia

5. HELLP (Hemolysis elevated liver enzymes low platelets) syndrome
   - 10-20% of preeclampsia
   - Hepatic hemorrhage, rupture or infarction in 45%
   - Presents with Hemolysis, elevated liver enzymes, low platelets
   - G1528C mutation has been associated

6. HELLP syndrome with subcapsular hematoma
   - If hemodynamically stable, then supportive management
   - Correct coagulopathy
   - Prophylactic antibiotic
   - Transfuse as needed
   - If patient with subcapsular hematoma is unstable then angiography or surgery
   - If liver failure, then transplantation

7. Acute fatty liver of pregnancy (AFLP)
   - Foetus have inherited mutation in mitochondrial oxidation of fatty acid (*LCHAD deficiency*)
   - Other deficiencies of fetoplacental mitochondrial oxidation associated with AFLP

- Short chain and medium chain acyl-CoA dehydrogenase deficiency
- Carnitine palmitoyltransferase deficiency
- Mitochondrial trifunctional protein deficiency

8. AFLP
- Presents with malaise, new onset nausea and vomiting, headache, jaundice in 3rd trimester
- Microvesicular steatosis
- Arginine vasopressin deficiency and central diabetes insipidus may occur
- Risks include multiple gestation, prior AFLP, male sex of fetus
- Develop acute liver failure with encephalopathy, hypocoagulopathy, hypoglycemia
- Management is prompt delivery of the fetus regardless of gestational age
- Test patients and their children for LCHAD and G158C mutation

9. AFLP vs HELLP
- Both in 3rd trimester
- AFLP presents with hypoglycemia, coagulopathy, increased creatinine
    - Babies have inherited mutation in mitochondrial oxidation of fatty acid (*LCHAD deficiency*)
- HELLP has hypertension -< 2% have LCHAD deficiency

10. Budd-Chiari syndrome (BCS) associated with postpartum period

11. Pregnancy with liver transplantation
- Safer *after 2 years* of transplantation
- High risk pregnancy
- AIH/viral hepatitis may aggravate with pregnancy
- Increase in acute cellular rejection and not ductopenic chronic rejection
- Add high dose steroids if any evidence of rejection
- Continue Tacrolimus (category C) if course is stable

12. Hepatitis B >200K during pregnancy then antiviral therapy should be started between 28-32 weeks
- IVIg and Hepatitis B virus (HBV) vaccine for the newborn

13. Ribavarin is teratogenic and in men conception should be deferred for at least 6 months after treatment
- Mycophenolate should be stopped at least 6 weeks before conception

Drug Induced Liver Injury (DILI)

1. Risk factors for DILI
    - Age> 60
    - Female
    - Obesity
    - Alcohol use
    - Prior DILI
    - *Cirrhosis does NOT increase the risk of DILI*

2. R factor is used to differentiate hepatocellular and cholestatic DILI
    - Uses ALT and ALP
    - < 2 is cholestatic pattern
    - > 5 is hepatocellular pattern
    - Between 2-5 is mixed pattern
    - Idiosyncratic DILI cases should be categorized by the R value at presentation (R =(ALT/ ULN)/(ALP/ULN)) into hepatocellular (R ≥ 5), mixed (2 < R < 5), and cholestatic (R ≤ 2) (AASLD 2022)

3. In individuals with suspected hepatocellular or mixed DILI exclude
    - Hepatitis A, B, and C and AIH with serologies and HCV RNA testing
    - Anti-HEV IgM testing in selected patients
    - Testing for acute CMV, Epstein-Barr virus, or acute HSV infection
    - Wilson disease and Budd-Chiari syndrome (BCS) when clinically appropriate

4. Three main types of hepatotoxicity with DILI (AASLD 2022)
    - Direct hepatotoxins (APAP) once a threshold is exceeded
    - Idiosyncratic DILI is independent of the dose and duration
        - Aberrant adaptive host immune response
    - Indirect hepatotoxins involve biological action of the drug on the liver and/ or host immune system
        - Independent of the dose and duration

5. Clinically significant DILI
    - Serum AST or ALT >5× ULN, or ALP >2× ULN (or pretreatment baseline if baseline is abnormal) on two separate occasions
    - Total serum bilirubin >2.5 mg/dl along with elevated AST, ALT, or ALP level
    - INR >1.5 with elevated AST, ALT, or ALP
    - Most hepatotoxic drugs cause DILI within the first 6 months

6. Increased risk for adverse outcomes in patients with DILI

- Higher bilirubin and INR values
- Lower serum albumin at presentation
- Severe necrosis and fibrosis
- Medical comorbidities
- Preexisting liver disease

7. Acetaminophen toxicity
    - >7.5 g
    - Lower dose with chronic Alcohol use
    - n-Acetylcysteine IV in encephalopathy 2 otherwise PO
    - Charcoal in Tylenol toxicity within 4 hours. Activated charcoal not helpful after a few hours

8. When to refer Tylenol toxicity patients for liver transplantation (UNOS criteria)
    - Encephalopathy
    - INR> 2
    - Renal replacement therapy
    - Vent dependent

9. Tylenol with elevated AST/ALT, normal Tylenol levels but with encephalopathy, refer to a liver transplant center

10. Tylenol toxicity
    - Toxic metabolite is n-acetyl p-benzoquinone imine (NAPQI) and is detoxified by glutathione
    - If n-Acetyl cysteine (NAC) is given within 15 hours then no liver toxicity. Likelihood of recovery is very high
    - Single important factor with Tylenol overdose is NAC within 8 hours
    - Alcohol increases the production of NAPQI
    - Level of transaminitis is NOT related to toxicity

11. Poor outcomes to Tylenol toxicity
    - Creatinine > 3.4
    - Encephalopathy 3 or 4
    - INR> 6.5
    - pH< 7.3

12. Tylenol with overdose with no detected Tylenol, still treat with NAC IV
    - Alcohol and Tylenol use > 2 days ago, still start NAC
    - Young male with increased AST and ALT in the 1000's check for Tylenol level

13. Tylenol toxicity with alcohol
    - Upregulation of CYP2E!

- Acute Alcohol intake may be protective. Discontinuation of alcohol increases the Tylenol metabolism towards toxic metabolite due to lack of competition

14. APAP causes acute pericentral liver injury
    - Leading cause of ALF among adults
    - Gastric lavage and activated charcoal within 4 h
    - IV or oral NAC can prevent liver injury if given within 12 h
    - Also recommended for patients presenting later
    - Prognosis related to encephalopathy, coagulopathy, acidosis

15. Drugs causing cholestasis
    - Augmentin (commonest DILI)
    - Anabolic steroids
    - Chlorpromazine and other Phenothiazines
    - Clopidogrel
    - OCP's
    - Erythromycin
    - Tricyclics
    - Irbesartan

16. Augmentin causes cholestatic jaundice
    - Commonest DILI
    - Self-resolving
    - Idiosyncratic
    - Can occur after the drug is stopped
    - May have eosinophilia or rash
    - Antibiotics and NSAIDS commonly cause of DILI

17. Patient with cholestasis and pruritus from Augmentin
    - Treat with cholestyramine
    - Rifampin
    - Naloxone/ Naltrexone

18. DILI with cholestasis usually never leads to acute liver failure

19. Cholestasis due to OTC medications
    - Resolves in 6-8 months
    - Monitor liver enzymes q2-4 weeks
    - Rarely progresses to liver failure

20. If patient taking supplements with elevated T Bili with normal liver chemistries and normal examination
    - Stop the supplements

- Chinese herb with cholestasis
    - Self-limited
    - Cholestatic pattern less likely to cause liver failure
    - Can last up to 6 weeks

21. In individuals with suspected cholestatic DILI:
    - Abdominal imaging
    - Serological testing for PBC with no obvious biliary tract pathology
    - Limit ERCP to instances where MRI or EUS is unable to exclude common bile duct stones, PSC, or pancreaticobiliary malignancy

22. DILI associated chronic liver injury (>6–12 months) in 10%–20% and cholestatic

23. Liver biopsy in DILI
    - If immunosuppressive therapy for suspected Autoimmune hepatitis (AIH) is contemplated
    - Rise in liver biochemistries or signs of worsening liver function despite stopping the offending agent
        - Peak ALT level has not fallen by >50% at 30–60 days in cases of hepatocellular DILI
        - Peak ALP has not fallen by >50% at 180 days in cases of cholestatic DILI
    - Continued use/ re-exposure to the implicated agent is contemplated
    - Liver biochemistry abnormalities persist beyond 180 days, especially if symptomatic

24. Scoring systems that include RUCAM should not be used as a sole diagnostic tool

25. Drug induced AIH
    - Nitrofurantoin
    - Minocyclin
    - Hydralazine
    - Diclofenac
    - Methyldopa
    - Statins
    - Infliximab

26. Acute liver toxicity due to drugs (other than Tylenol) has a high case fatality rate.
    - Transplant center/ transplantation right away

27. Statins are safe to use in cirrhosis

- Statins cause idiosyncratic hepatotoxicity
- Statins with elevated liver enzymes, continue statin since there is a process of adaptation and may normalize. Alternatively, a different statin may not elevate liver enzymes.
- Zetia (Ezetimibe) reduces cholesterol in liver disease
- PBC with increase cholesterol (not triglycerides) doesn't increase cardiovascular risks and doesn't need treatment
- Omega-3 fatty acids are not helpful in liver disease to reduce triglycerides

28. Predose liver tests in all patients initiating statin therapy
    - No routine labs even in patients with liver disease
    - No contraindications for statins in compensated cirrhosis
    - Statins in decompensated cirrhosis should be individualized

29. Young patient with valproic acid toxicity
    - Decoupling of oxidative phosphorylation in mitochondria
    - Microvesicular steatosis without inflammation
    - Mild elevation of AST and ALT though patient has liver failure
    - Valproic acid associated liver failure has normal LFTs and T Bili but increased ammonia and INR with lethargy
    - Treated with Carnitine

30. INH toxicity and IV NAC
    - In patients presenting with non–acetaminophen-associated ALF, NAC only in the context of clinical trials (AGA 2017)
    - INH with liver failure with encephalopathy and elevated INR treated with IV NAC
    - Centrilobular necrosis in INH toxicity
    - With normal INR and no encephalopathy, manage conservatively

31. Daily significant alcohol use, on Levetiracetam (Keppra) for seizures and very high elevated liver enzymes and T Bili
    - Levetiracetam not metabolized by liver and safe in cirrhosis
    - Not HCV even if anti-HCV + (doesn't cause very high liver enzymes)
    - Start IV NAC due to accidental Tylenol use suspected

32. Metoclopramide increases Tacrolimus and Cyclosporine levels
    - Protease inhibitors for HCV may increase levels
    - Patient on tacrolimus for several years with increased creatinine and tacrolimus level pending- STOP Tacrolimus

33. Drugs more likely to cause DILI in older individuals
    - Amoxicillin-clavulanate

- Isoniazid

34. Drugs more likely to cause DILI in children
    - Valproate
    - Minocycline

35. Pre-existing liver disease are at increased risk of DILI with
    - Methotrexate
    - Anti-TB therapy
    - Poor outcomes

36. Herbal and dietary supplements (HDS) account for an increasing proportion of DILI due to bodybuilding and weight loss supplements
    - Apply the same diagnostic approach for DILI to suspected HDS-hepatotoxicity
    - Stop all HDS in patients with suspected HDS-hepatotoxicity
    - Consider liver transplantation evaluation in patients who develop ALF and severe cholestatic injury from HDS-DILI

37. The presence of eosinophils/granulomas on a liver biopsy in DILI is associated with a better outcome than necrosis/fibrosis

38. Fialuridine is a mitochondrial toxin that led to microvesicular steatosis and necrosis

39. NASH with decompensation
    - No increased risk of DILI
    - Avoid NSAIDS
    - Tylenol in recommended doses is safe since the production of toxic NAPQI is slower

40. Patients with cirrhosis have no increased risk of DILI
    - Tylenol is safe in recommended doses
    - NSAIDS avoided in cirrhosis due to increased nephrotoxicity

41. Large cavernous blood-filled spaces in liver is Peliosis hepatis which is associated with
    - Azathioprine
    - OCP
    - Steroids
    - Cyclosporine
    - Bartonella
    - TB
    - HIV and Immune disorders

42. The outcomes of idiosyncratic DILI are relatively favorable, with only

~ 10% reaching the threshold of ALF < 20% developing chronic liver injury.

43. Acute liver failure (ALF) patients always treated with IV NAC
    - In patients presenting with non–acetaminophen-associated ALF, the AGA recommends that NAC only be used in the context of clinical trials (AGA 2021)
    - No testing for Wilson's
    - Test for HSV and ANA
    - In pregnant women test for hepatitis E
    - No liver biopsy
    - No empiric treatment to reduce intracranial pressure

44. Patient with increased AST> 3N on immune checkpoint inhibitors for cancer. Stop the checkpoint inhibitor.
    - Steroids only with jaundice

45. Sinusoidal dilatation on liver biopsy consistent with OCP and BCS

46. DILI that results in ALF carries a poor prognosis
    - 40% requiring liver transplantation and 42% dying of the episode
    - Advanced coma grade and high MELD scores are associated with poor outcomes

47. Use a prognostic model consisting of MELD, Charlson comorbidity index, and serum albumin in clinical practice for predicting 6-month mortality in DILI.

48. Avoid re-exposure to a drug if the initial liver injury was associated with significant AST elevation (e.g., >5xULN or jaundice)
    - Stop suspected agent(s) in DILI, especially when liver biochemistries are rising rapidly or there is evidence of liver dysfunction
    - Consider NAC treatment in adults with early-stage ALF, given some evidence for efficacy in early coma stage patients
    - NO NAC for children with severe DILI leading to ALF
    - Corticosteroid therapy equivocal in DILI. However, they may be considered in DILI exhibiting AIH-like features

49. Patients with chronic HBV and HCV may be more prone to develop liver injury due to specific agents such as isoniazid and antiretrovirals

50. Obeticholic acid associated with hepatic decompensation in patients with PBC and Child-Pugh class B and C cirrhosis who received a higher than recommended dose.

51. HLA-B 35:01 causes hepatotoxicity to green tea extract in Whites
    - P. multiflorum hepatotoxicity in Asians

52. Idiosyncratic DILI with acute liver injury resolves within 6m
    - 10% of idiosyncratic DILI have ALF, Ltx, and death
    - Low survival 25%
    - Early transfer to a liver transplant center

53. Rx of idiosyncratic DILI (AASLD 2022)
    - Stop suspect drug
    - Supportive care of antiemetics, antipruritics, and hydration
    - Intravenous NAC in hospitalized adult (not kids) with ALF
    - Corticosteroids x 1–3 months in severe hypersensitivity features, Drug reaction eosinophilia and systemic symptoms (DRESS), and autoimmune features on liver biopsy
    - URSO not an established therapy for DILI but is presumably safe

54. Defibrotide is a profibrolytic in moderate to severe VOD/ Sinusoidal obstructive syndrome (SOS)

55. Rechallenge with the suspect drug avoided

56. High-risk drugs for hepatotoxicity are
    - Immune checkpoint inhibitors (ICI)
    - Isoniazid
    - Methotrexate

57. Elevations of liver enzymes in INH can be self-limited, presumably because of metabolic and immunological adaptation

58. Annual measurement of liver elastography in methotrexate

59. Predosing and on-treatment labs is the standard of care for ICIs
    - Withhold drug, increase lab test, and use of corticosteroids

60. Acute on Chronic Liver Failure and DILI
    - When DILI causes liver injury, usually causes acute liver failure.
    - Incidence in Asian countries is 10%, US~ 7%
    - DILI in advanced liver disease has poor outcome.
    - ACLF occurs ~1 month after medication, but up to 3 months.
    - Mortality in DILI-related ACLF is >50%, with the ACLF grade as the only significant predictor of mortality.

Tumors and Miscellaneous

1. Hepatoma
    - Alpha-fetoprotein (AFP) not recommended for screening
    - AST/ALT> 1 indicative of cirrhosis
    - MRI shows arterial enhancement follow by portal venous washout
    - HCC screening in HCV with bridging fibrosis and cirrhosis
    - Cigarette smoking, IL28BTT also increases the risk of HCC

2. Most of the world's HCC is in subsaharan Africa/ Asia

3. Radiology criteria for HCC
    - Major:
        - Non-rim-like arterial phase hyperenhancement
        - Non-Peripheral washout (delayed washout)
        - Enhancing capsule (pseudocapsule)
        - Size > 20 mm
        - Threshold growth >50% increase in 6 months
    - Minor:
        - Nodule in nodule
        - Non-enhancing capsule
        - Mosaic
        - Blood products within the lesion
        - Fat in the lesion

4. Triple phase CT with enhancing lesion in arterial phase and venous washout is consistent with HCC
    - Patients with cirrhosis and tumor occlusion of portal vein can develop ALF with chemoembolization of HCC

5. Cirrhosis + ascites with elevated AFP and portal vein clot and negative MRI, triple phase CT to evaluate for HCC
    - MRI is poor with ascites
    - New onset portal vein clot should trigger w/u to r/o HCC

6. Highest risk of HCC is HBV and HCV coinfection
    - Treat HCC (liver transplant etc.) before treatment of HCV with antivirals
    - HCC with macroscopic vascular invasion is a contraindication for liver transplantation
    - Management of resectable HCC in decompensated cirrhosis is Liver transplantation

7. Milan criteria for liver transplantation in HCC is single lesion < 5 cm and 3 lesions less than 3 cm

8. UCSF criteria for transplantation
- Tumor < 6.5 cm
- 2-3 tumors largest < 4.5 with total tumor burden of 8 cm

9. Systemic therapy for advanced hepatocellular carcinoma (HCC). ie. HCC with stable liver function not eligible for locoregional therapies (LRT) or resection or with metastatic disease, atezolizumab+bevacizumab over sorafenib.
- First line is Atezolizumab + Bevacizumab
    - EGD before Bevacizumab therapy due to increased risk of bleeding varices
- Second line is Sorafenib and Lenvatinib
- Alternate therapies are
    - Regorafenib, Cabozantinib
    - Nivolumab, Pembrolizumab, Ramucirumab (not for first line therapy failure)
        - Ramucirumab only if AFP >400 ng/mL
    - HCC with preserved liver function and progression of disease on sorafenib, then cabozantinib, pembrolizumab, regorafenib over no systemic therapy

10. Atezolizumab + Bevacizumab better than sorafenib for advanced HCC. Lenvatinib also better than sorafenib

11. Vertical transmission of HBV increases the risk of HCC x 100
- Level of HBV correlates to risk of cancer
- Can cause HCC without cirrhosis
- Alcohol and Aflatoxin increases the risk even further
- HBV vaccine decrease the incidence of HCC

12. Hemochromatosis with cirrhosis are at a risk of HCC
- Portal vein clot may need triple phase CT to rule out HCC.
    - Hereditary Hemochromatosis (HH) who develop bleeding esophageal varices with US showing PV thrombus. Next step triple phase CT to r/o HCC
- If homozygous for Hemochromatosis gene, then check spouse's DNA to evaluate risk to children
- Commonest cause of death in HH is HCC

13. Portal vein clot progressing to SMV clots treat with anticoagulation except in case of tumor thrombus

14. Young patient with fibrolamellar liver cancer, treatment is surgical

resection with LN dissection.
- Normal liver enzymes and normal AFP

15. HCC Screening
- Asian women > 50 years
- Asian men > 40 years
- African adults
- Coinfection of HBV and HDV
- First degree relatives with HCC

16. PSC 30-year risk of cholangiocarcinoma is 20%.
- PSC stricture brushing are needed to rule out cholangiocarcinoma
- Need annual colonoscopy in IBD patients with 32 biopsies

17. Cholangioca can be considered for transplantation if
- Tumor < 3 cm
- No mets
- No percutaneous biopsies

18. Cholangiocarcinoma metastatic treated with gemcitabine and cisplatin

19. Hypervascular metastases in Breast cancer, Lung, NET, Thyroid, Melanoma
- Hypovascular metastasis in Breast cancer, Pancreas, Colon, Lung

20. Patient with lymphoma, check for HCV
- Elderly male with increased ALP with normal or low AST and ALT with weight loss and liver enlargement has Lymphoma
- DD includes sarcoidosis, amyloidosis and fungal hepatitis

21. Central scar in a liver mass that enhances on MRI hepatic arterial phase is an Focal Nodular Hyperplasia (FNH)
- Due to local vascular insult with hypertrophy
- No follow up scanning unless atypical
- Symptomatic large FNH needs surgery
- MRI with Eovist retention is seen in FNH
- Liver lesion with central scar is FNH and requires no follow up

22. Nodular regenerative hyperplasia
- Middle aged patient with nodular liver with history of SLE x 20 years with normal liver chemistry with negative liver tests
- Vascular injury to the liver
- Associated with systemic autoimmune disorders
- Nodularity may cause portal hypertension

- Screen for HCC q 2 years in patients with cirrhosis
- Check hepatic vein pressure gradient measurement. If less than 5 mm then no cirrhosis and no surveillance

23. Sinusoidal obstruction syndrome (SOS)
    - Venoocclusive disease
    - Post sinusoidal portal hypertension in the setting of myeloablative chemotherapy with or without total body irradiation
    - URSO prescribed the day before chemoablation and continuing x 3 months for prevention
    - Defibrotide x 14 days is the only FDA approved medication
        - Single stranded poly deoxyribonucleic acid with fibrinolytic and anti ischemic properties
    - Histology shows zone 3 congestion with hemorrhage and collagen deposition with nonthrombotic occlusion of central veins and sinusoids
    - Microthrombi in hepatic vessels, Hepatomegaly, Jaundice, Ascites

24. Hepatic adenoma >/= 5 cm has increased risk of HCC
    - Large lesions, growing lesions (>20% in 6 months), beta catenin positive lesions, exophytic lesions need surgery
    - Enhancing mass with washout and no central scar and no rim enhancement
    - On MRI with contrast arterial phase enhancement without washout or central scar
    - Stop OCP/steroids

25. Ground glass appearance of hepatocytes is HBV managed by entecavir

26. Asymptomatic simple liver cysts managed by observation alone

27. Large symptomatic liver cyst treated by alcohol ablation. If not successful then surgical fenestration

Cirrhosis

1. New cirrhotic with AST/ ALT > 1 and reduced platelet counts
   - Check for varices. Grade B or greater varices treated with non-specific beta blockers

2. Mallory bodies are Eosinophilic hyaline on liver biopsy
   - Alcohol
   - Amiodarone
   - Tamoxifen
   - Wilson's disease
   - Non-alcoholic steatohepatitis (NASH)
   - Jejunoileal bypass

3. NSAIDS, ACE inhibitors and ACE blockers should be avoided in patients with cirrhosis and ascites (AASLD 2021)
   - Aminoglycosides should be avoided whenever possible in the treatment of bacterial infections

4. Spur cell anemia caused by fatty liver - cholesterol and fats damage red cell membrane

5. Ascitic Fluid - Low protein and High Serum ascites albumin gradient (SAAG) is Cirrhosis
   - High protein and High SAAG is CHF
     - Patients with JVP, Rales, increased ascites protein, increased SAAG is Alcohol induced CHF, constrictive pericarditis etc
     - Protein > 2.5 g/dl in ascitic fluid indicates cardiac source
     - High SAAG, high protein ascitic fluid with increase hepatic vein wedge pressure and high free hepatic vein pressure with normal gradient
     - Echocardiogram may be normal in constrictive pericarditis so use CT or MRI

6. Acute BCS presents with RUQ pain along with ascites and reduced SAAG (initially)
   - Ascites associated with Nephrotic syndrome has SAAG < 1.1 and protein < 2.5

7. Carvedilol max dose is 12.5 mg/ day. Higher doses will cause impaired metabolism and hypotension

8. Cirrhotic patients' diet

- Protein 1.2-1.5 g/kg
- Late night snack
- High carb diet not recommended
- PO (not IV) branched chain amino acid diet
- Muscle wasting with cirrhosis and encephalopathy: Add a late night snack

9. Patient with refractory ascites
    - Treat with TIPS if no encephalopathy and MELD is low
    - Before TIPS r/o pulmonary HTN and LV dysfunction with echocardiogram
    - r/o HCC and BCS with doppler US

10. Ascites with cloudy fluid but no infection, with increased triglycerides and low protein in ascitic fluid with increased SAAG. 20% of patients with Cirrhosis have chylous ascites
    - Patient with SAAG> 1.1, T protein in fluid > 1.5, increased triglycerides has Alcoholic cirrhosis with seepage of lymph from Glisson's capsule

11. Pregnancy is rare in individuals with well-compensated cirrhosis due to anovulatory cycles

12. Refractory ascites with increased creatinine - stop propranolol (beta-blockers)

13. Polycystic liver disease check MRI of the brain for aneurysm

14. Refractory ascites - stop beta-blockers (perhaps stop ACE inhibitors)

15. A patient with a MELD score below 10 can undergo elective surgery, whereas caution needs to be exercised for a patient with a MELD score of 10-15. For patients with a MELD score above 15 elective surgery is risky
    - Surgery of any type in cirrhosis is associated with Acute on Chronic Liver Failure (ACLF)
        - Use Mayo Clinic score/ VOCAL PENN score
    - Hepatic decompensation and infection are risk factors for the development of ACLF after surgery
    - Higher risk of ACLF with ERCP in severe liver disease

16. INR not increasing with warfarin, diet to blame

17. Vibration controlled transient elastography (VCTE) and cirrhosis (AGA 2017)
    - Chronic HCV and chronic alcoholic liver disease, VCTE 12.5 kPa
    - Noncirrhotic patients with HCV, VCTE of 9.5 kPa to r/o advanced fibrosis

- Chronic Hepatitis B, VCTE cutoff of 11.0 kPa
- No recommendation regarding the role of VCTE in the diagnosis of cirrhosis in adults with Nonalcoholic fatty liver disease (NAFLD). MRE, rather than VCTE, for detection of cirrhosis
- Compensated cirrhosis, VCTE cutoff of 19.5 kPa to assess the need for EGD to identify high risk esophageal varices.
- Chronic liver disease undergoing elective non hepatic surgery, VCTE cutoff of 17.0 kPa to detect clinically significant portal hypertension

18. Palliative care in decompensated Cirrhosis (DC) (AASLD 2022)
    - Palliative care provided to patients with DC at any stage
    - Does not preclude the delivery curative treatments such as transplantation evaluation
    - Outpatient palliative care associated with improved symptoms, care coordination, and anticipatory planning
    - Greater consensus about the goals of care
    - Reduced life-sustaining treatment use
    - Earlier provision of comfort-focused care
    - Reduced readmission
    - Abdominal drains may be an alternative to serial LVP for refractory ascites whose goals are comfort focused

19. Pain in cirrhosis
    - Acetaminophen, 500 mg every 6 h, to a max dose of 2 g/d
    - Systemic NSAIDs should be avoided
    - Avoiding opioids for chronic pain.

20. Cirrhosis and dyspnea
    - Nonpharmacological therapies include the use of a fan, supplemental oxygen (even for nonhypoxic patients), and mindfulness exercises
    - Opioids and anxiolytics

21. Cirrhosis and muscle cramps
    - Checking serum electrolyte levels and repleting potassium, magnesium, and zinc is a first step
    - Taurine (2–3 g daily), vitamin E (200 mg three times a day), and baclofen (5–10 mg three times a day)

22. Melatonin improves sleep quality in cirrhotics

22. First-line for nausea and vomiting is ondansetron (maximum 8 mg/d), using caution given constipating effects
    - Medical marijuana is not first-line management for any symptom for patients with DC.

23. MELD >21 and Child-Pugh >12 is when patients are prognostically appropriate for hospice (i.e., have estimated survival of ≤6 months)

24. Acute on Chronic liver failure (ACLF) (ACG 2022)
   - Hospitalized patients with ACLF, short-acting dexmedetomidine for sedation to shorten time to extubation
   - No liver transplantation in Cirrhosis+ACLF who require mechanical ventilation because of brain or respiratory failure

25. Cirrhosis and respiratory system
   - In ventilated patients no prophylactic antibiotics
   - Endotracheal intubation is mandatory in grade 3–4 HE
   - The risk of ventilation-associated pneumonia can be decreased by 30- to 45-degree head-end elevation and subglottic suction.
   - Routine use of sedatives is discouraged in grade 3–4 HE and may be associated with delay in extubating.
   - PPIs in patients with cirrhosis on a ventilator.
   - Higher mean arterial blood pressure (MAP) may decrease ACLF
   - Norepinephrine is the vasopressor of choice in ACLF.

26. Vaccinate chronic liver patients against hepatitis A and B

27. 5% albumin for rapid volume resuscitation, whereas 25% for sustained volume expansion
   - Benefits of artificial liver support systems unclear.
   - Plasma exchange improves survival in acute liver failure; unknown in ACLF
   - In cirrhosis and ACLF, no granulocyte colony-stimulating factor (G-CSF) to improve mortality. G-CSF reduces short-term mortality in Asia but not in Western cohorts or in children

28. Hepatic encephalopathy with liver cirrhosis (ISHEN 2020)
   - If ammonia is normal then alternative source of encephalopathy to be evaluated
   - Treat the underlying precipitating cause
   - Isolated elevation of ammonia without clinical signs of encephalopathy is not an indication of therapy
   - Lactulose, Rifaximin, Branched-chain aminoacid for preventing recurrent episodes of hepatic encephalopathy
   - Acute episode treated by Lactulose, Polyethylene glycol if not tolerating lactulose, IV L-ornithine-L-aspartate (LOLA)
   - Cognitive testing alone should not be used to restrict driving
   - Oral and written advice to avoid driving in patients with recent (< 3 months) encephalopathy
   - Diagnosis of covert (minimal) hepatic encephalopathy based on

nationally validated neuropsychological tests

29. Encephalopathy that doesn't respond to lactulose, add Rifaximin

30. Encephalitis with muscle wasting in cirrhosis, treat with late night snacks

31. SBP prophylaxis
    - GI Bleed with ascites
    - Previous SBP
    - Low protein <1.5 g/dL and either bilirubin >3 + Child Pugh Score >9
    - Low protein with low Na, elevated creatinine or BUN

32. Traumatic ascitic tap
    - Treat with antibiotics
    - Polymicrobial
    - PMN< 250

33 Cirrhosis and infections
    - Always assess for infection
    - In suspected infection early treatment with antibiotics
        - Antibiotics de-escalated once cultures are available
    - In decompensated cirrhosis nosocomial infection is associated with increased risk of ACLF and mortality.
    - Cirrhotics at significant risk of nosocomial & fungal infections
    - Fungal infection has increased risk of ACLF and mortality

34. Antibiotics for secondary SBP prophylaxis to prevent recurrence
    - Daily prophylactic antibiotics; no specific regimen is superior
    - PPI use increases infection, avoid unless clear indication
    - Beta-blockers may decrease bacterial translocation
    - Rifaximin may prevent cirrhosis complication other than HE

35. Fibrosis staging done at diagnosis and during follow-up
    - Liver stiffness (LS) measurement by TE or MRE
    - Liver biopsy is not recommended for fibrosis staging
    - EGD for varices screen if the LS is >20 kPa by TE or the platelet count is ≤150,000/mm3.

Cirrhosis and Hepatic Circulation

1. Cirrhosis has normal free hepatic venous pressure but elevated wedge pressure and elevated hepatic venous pressure gradient
   - Hepatic being pressure gradient > 20 associated with variceal bleed

2. Extrahepatic portal vein thrombosis shows normal wedge and Free hepatic vein pressure as well as normal gradient
   - Isolated portal vein thrombosis does NOT cause ascites

3. Cardiac causes such as constrictive pericarditis has increase hepatic vein wedge pressure and high free hepatic vein pressure with normal gradient
   - Right heart failure and BCS develop ascites and not variceal bleed
   - In Budd-Chiari syndrome (BCS) the pressure are all low

4. Patient with hypotension and increased liver enzymes is shock liver
   - Increasing T Bili, decreasing INR and Improving liver enzymes that were in the thousands indicates vascular injury
   - T Bili elevations occurs 3-5 days after transaminase peak
   - Diagnosis with US of liver with doppler

5. Procoagulant that is increased in cirrhosis and causes thrombosis in factor VIII.
   - Protein C that is a natural anticoagulant is also reduced in cirrhosis

6. Patient with portal vein clot and cavernous transformation- esophageal varices banded and repeat banding in 4 weeks

7. CT of the abdomen in patient with hepatitis cirrhosis shows a portal vein clot that enhances in arterial phase, management is MRI next

8. Dilated hepatic veins like a maple leaf is right heart failure

9. Air in portal vein is ischemic bowel

10. Pneumatosis linearis indicates ischemia in bowel wall (CT angiogram needed)

11. Chemotherapy can cause non-cirrhotic portal hypertension
    - On chemotherapy
    - Hx of cirrhosis with normal albumin
    - Normal liver enzymes
    - Ascites with Increased SAAG

- Not cirrhosis since albumin is normal but non-cirrhotic portal hypertension caused by chemotherapy

12. Budd Chiari syndrome (BCS)
    - Hepatic vein thrombosis: spider veins like collaterals on venogram
    - Increase SAAG with high protein in BCS (acute BCS, decreased SAAG)
    - Absence of hepatojugular reflux
    - Caudate lobe has direct veins emptying into the IVC and gets hypertrophied.
    - BCS has low Free hepatic vein pressure
    - Histologically zone 3 central venous congestion and dilation of sinusoids
    - BCS treated with IV Heparin, SQ low molecular weight heparin and TIPS.

13. Management of BCS
    - Check for 2 or more thrombotic conditions. Look for additional causes even if one obvious risk factor is present
    - Referral to a hematologist to work up prothrombotic conditions
        - Increased risk in factor V Leiden and Myeloproliferative disorders
    - Doppler in chronic liver disease in the event of new onset ascites or abdominal pain
    - Balloon angioplasty of hepatic vein clots only if short segments are affected
    - Covered stents better than uncovered stents for TIPS
    - US guided direct intrahepatic porta-systemic shunt (DIPS) when TIPS not feasible
    - Surgery when DIPS or TIPS not feasible
    - Patients receiving liver transplant for BSC need to be considered for long term anticoagulation

14. Surveillance for HCC every 6 months in patients with chronic BCS.
    - Commonest cause in Asia and Africa is membranous obstruction of IVC
    - Commonest cause in West is hepatic vein thrombosis

15. Young patients with portal vein clot and cavernous transformation with no cirrhosis are prehepatic portal hypertension. Treatment is band varices

16. CT scan or MRI/MRCP in patients with symptomatic Hereditary hemorrhagic telangiectasia (HHT) with liver vascular malformations
    - Doppler US is less accurate in patients with HHT and symptomatic Liver vascular malformations (LVM)
    - Standard medical therapy for each complication of liver VMs in patients with HHT, which results in symptom resolution in the majority.
    - Bevacizumab should be considered in patients with high output heart failure (HOHF) and possibly for other complications of LVM

- Liver transplant is an important option for nonresponders but may be associated with a high rate of complications, and liver VMs may recur as early as 6 years after transplant

17. Cirrhosis with large non-bleeding varices. Beta Blockers not tolerated. Treat with variceal ligation

18. Cirrhosis and homeostasis (ACG 2020)
    - In well compensated cirrhosis the homeostatic pathways are largely intact but in precarious balance
    - The decrease in procoagulants is balanced by loss of liver generated anticoagulants and increased endothelial derived factor VIII and vWF
    - Conventional tests do not detect relative hypercoagulability of liver disease
    - Whole blood viscoelastic tests such as TEG and ROTEM may be better at assessing coagulation
    - Pharmacologic therapy for DVT prophylaxis is safe in cirrhotics without bleeding or platelets < 50 k

19. Thrombosis of mesenteric and portal veins in patients with or without cirrhosis (ACG 2020)
    - Thrombophilia workup in the absence of cirrhosis or acute abdominal process
        - In cirrhotic patients when there is previous history or family history of thrombosis or in unusual sites such as hepatic veins
    - Check for JAK2 mutation indicating myeloproliferative disorder which the commonest cause of thrombophilia
    - Doppler US of liver vasculature recommended in new onset cirrhosis, onset of portal hypertension or decompensation
    - Anticoagulation for thrombosis in cirrhosis is not associated with increased variceal bleed

20. Anticoagulation for patients with chronic portal vein thrombosis if there is (ACG 2020)
    - Evidence of inherited or acquired thrombophilia
    - Progression of thrombus into the mesenteric veins
    - Current or previous evidence of bowel ischemia
    - 6 months of anticoagulation
        - Indefinite anticoagulation is recommended in patients with portal or mesenteric vein thrombosis and thrombophilia
    - Low molecular weight heparin (LMWH) or warfarin only
        - Currently only limited experience with DOAC because absorption of these agents may be limited in the presence of intestinal edema
    - Risk of bleeding must be weighed against benefits in patients with

platelets <50,000/μL or hepatic encephalopathy at risk of falls

21. Six months of anticoagulation in patients with cirrhosis and acute portal or Mesenteric Vein Thrombosis.
   - Anticoagulation is continued beyond this period in patients who are on liver transplant
   - Unfractionated heparin is preferred in the presence of renal insufficiency
   - LMWH is preferred in the presence of thrombocytopenia

22. Asymptomatic mesenteric artery aneurysms <2 cm
   - Only with aneurysms of the pancreaticoduodenal and gastroduodenal arcade, intraparenchymal hepatic artery branches
   - Follow-up imaging in 6 months, then at 1 year and subsequently every 1–2 years.
   - Treat Mesenteric artery aneurysms associated with symptoms
   - Treat all aneurysms >2 cm in diameter even when asymptomatic
   - Women of childbearing age
   - Recipients of a liver transplant

23. Cirrhosis and coagulation
   - No INR to measure coagulation risk
   - There is an increased risk of venous thromboembolism (VTE), hospitalized cirrhotics need pharmacologic VTE prophylaxis
   - No transfusions for altered coagulation parameters in the absence of bleeding or a planned procedure
   - Thromboelastography (TEG) or rotational TEG (ROTEM) over INR to assess transfusion needs for invasive procedures
   - Hypocoagulation found on TEG/ROTEM in ACLF is an independent marker of poor prognosis and is usually found in patients with SIRS
   - In well-controlled decompensated cirrhosis, low-molecular-weight heparin may decrease the risk of new decompensation

Cirrhosis and Alcohol

1. Alcoholic liver disease if lack of response to steroids in 7 days, then stop steroids

2. Alcohol liver disease for surgery, NSAIDS are avoided, if opiates given no APAP

3. Alcoholic liver disease - If Maddrey's score > 32 or MELD >20 (AASLD 2019), prednisolone
   - Discriminant function = (4.6 x PT diff +T Bili) DF> 32 or with hepatic encephalopathy
   - Prednisolone 40 mg QD x 4 weeks
       - Contraindicated in GI bleed or infection
   - The addition of intravenous NAC to prednisolone (40 mg/day) may improve the 30-day survival of patients with severe AH
   - The Lille score should be used to reassess prognosis, identify non-responders, and guide treatment course after 7 days of corticosteroids
   - No pentoxifylline

4. Patients with decompensated alcohol-associated cirrhosis, CPT class C or MELD-Na of at least 21 should be referred and considered for liver transplantation.
   - Liver transplantation is an option if no response after 7 days
   - Candidate selection for liver transplantation should not be based solely on a fixed interval of abstinence
   - Liver transplantation may be considered in carefully selected patients with favorable psychosocial profiles

5. Severe alcoholic hepatitis that did not respond to steroids have markedly improved survival with early liver transplantation

6. Alcoholic fatty liver to cirrhosis in 20% who continue to drink. Survival predicted by
   - PT/INR
   - Creatinine
   - T Bili
   - Hepatic encephalopathy
   - Albumin does NOT predict survival in alcoholic hepatitis.

7. Ballooning and Mallory bodies indicate alcoholic hepatitis

8. Isolated gastric varices (IGV1) with bleed, CT scan to evaluate splenic vein thrombosis

- Treat with splenectomy for recurrent bleed
- Cyanoacrylate glue for acute bleed

9. Splenic vein thrombosis managed by short interval imaging study over anticoagulation

10. FDA approved therapy for Alcohol use disorder (AUD)
    - Disulfiram
    - Naltrexone
    - Acamprosate (safe in acute hepatitis)
    - Baclofen (AASLD 2019)

11. Cirrhosis and Alcohol
    - Severe alcohol-associated hepatitis prednisolone/ prednisone improves 28-day mortality
        - Discriminant function ≥ 32; MELD> 20
    - Acute alcoholic hepatitis leads to ACLF as a result of a combination of a severe SIRS and sepsis.

12. Relapse after liver transplant for ETOH liver disease associated with
    - Lack of a partner/ spouse leads to ETOH relapse
    - Duration of sobriety before Ltx is associated with continued sobriety after LTx
    - > 10 drinks per day
    - Multiple previous rehab attempts
    - Prior alcohol associated legal issues
    - Illicit substance use

Cirrhosis and Acute Kidney Injury (AKI)

1. Diagnosis of AKI in Liver disease (AGA 2022)
   - Creatinine increases by ≥0.3 mg/dL within 48 hours or ≥50 percent from baseline
   - Urine output is reduced below 0.5 mL/kg/h for >6 hours

2. Causes of AKI
   - Hypovolemia (volume responsive and the most common)
   - Acute tubular necrosis
   - Hepatorenal syndrome with AKI (HRS-AKI) (Renal failure persists despite volume repletion)
   - HRS with acute kidney disease, a type of functional renal failure of <3 months – duration in which criteria for HRS-AKI are not met
   - Postrenal rarely

3. Prevention of AKI in cirrhosis
   - Avoidance of potentially nephrotoxic medications NSAIDs
   - Avoidance of excessive diuretics or nonselective beta-blockade
   - Avoidance of large-volume paracentesis without albumin
   - Avoid alcohol use

4. r/o infection in all patients with AKI
   - Diagnostic paracentesis for spontaneous bacterial peritonitis
   - Blood and urine cultures and Chest X-ray

5. No routine prophylactic antibiotics in patients with AKI, but broad-spectrum antibiotics when infection is strongly suspected

6. Treatment of AKI- Diuretics and nonselective beta-blockers held
   - NSAIDs discontinued
   - Precipitating cause of AKI treated
   - Fuid losses replaced
   - Albumin 1 g/kg/d for 2 days if creatinine x2 baseline

7. Vasoconstrictors for Hepatorenal syndrome (HRS)
   - Midodrine
   - Norepinephrine (only in ICU)
   - Terlipressin

8. Treatment of HRS-AKI
   - If creatinine remains >2 baseline despite standard treatment
   - Albumin at a dose of 1 g/kg intravenously on day 1 followed by 20-40 g daily

- Vasoactive agents
  - Terlipressin - bolus dose of 1 mg q4-6 hours and increased to 2 mg q4-6 hours if creatinine on day three is not lowered by at least 25% or
  - Terlipressin by IV infusion at 2 mg/d and increase the dose gradually
  - No terlipressin if creatinine ≥5 mg/dL, or O2 <90%
- Combination of octreotide SQ and Oral midodrine TID
- Norepinephrine continuous IV infusion with the goal of increasing the mean arterial pressure by ≥10 mm Hg and/or the urine output to >50 mL/h for at least 4 hours
- Continued x 14 days or 24 hours following creatinine level to within ≤0.3 mg/dL of baseline x 2 days

9. Ischemic side effects of terlipressin and norepinephrine include angina and ischemia of fingers, skin and intestine
   - Side effects lowered by starting low and gradual increase

10. Excessive use of albumin has a risk of pulmonary edema

11. Renal replacement therapy (RRT) may be used in the management of
    - AKI secondary to acute tubular necrosis
    - HRS-AKI in potential candidates for liver transplantation
    - RRT should not be used in patients with HRS-AKI who are not candidates for liver transplantation
    - AKI of uncertain etiology in which the need for RRT may be considered on an individual basis.

12. Liver transplantation is the most effective treatment for HRS-AKI
    - Pharmacotherapy for HRS-AKI before transplantation associated with better post-transplantation outcomes
    - Selected patients with HRS-AKI may require simultaneous liver kidney transplantation based on updated Organ Procurement and Transplantation Network listing criteria.

13. Alcoholic patient with increased creatinine and decreased urine sodium
    - Dehydration or prerenal
    - Hydrate for possible dehydration first
    - HRS diagnosis only after 1.5 liters of fluid bolus without improvement in urine output or creatinine

14. Cirrhosis Kidney disease
    - In stages 2 and 3 acute kidney injury (AKI), intravenous (IV) albumin + vasoconstrictors Over albumin alone, to improve creatinine
    - No biomarkers to predict the development of renal failure
    - High creatinine have worse renal outcomes and 30-day survival

15. HRS-AKI with**out** high grade ACLF give
    - Terlipressin or Norepinephrine

16. Cirrhosis and SBP, albumin+antibiotics to prevent AKI
    - Infections other than SBP No Albumin.
    - Kidney failure is the most common organ failure in ACLF
    - No vasoconstrictors for stage 1 AKI.
    - Refer for LT assessment early in the course of AKI.

Cirrhosis and Transplantation

1. Transplant evaluation for MELD> 17
    - Patient with refractory ascites and MELD of 23 - send for transplant evaluation

2. MELD uses serum creatinine, INR and Bilirubin. Sodium used in MELD-Na

3. MELD priority (Exceptions)
    - Hyperoxaluria - patients need Kidney + Liver transplantation
    - Familial amyloid
    - Cystic fibrosis
    - Hilar cholangiocarcinoma
    - Hepatic artery thrombosis after surgery
    - HCC
    - Hepatopulmonary syndrome with arterial Po2 < 60
    - Portopulmonary hypertension < 35 mm. Has poor post transplant outcomes

4. Contraindications to liver transplantation
    - Pulmonary hypertension
    - Intrahepatic cholangiocarcinoma
    - BMI> 40
    - Hemangiosarcoma
    - HCC with macroscopic vascular invasion

5. Hepatopulmonary syndrome recovery can take up to 1 year following liver transplantation

6. Fever, leukopenia, systemic symptoms within 6 weeks of liver transplantation is CMV virus.
    - Most common infection after transplantation is CMV. Diagnosed by CMV PCR
    - CMV infections common 3-12 months after liver transplantation

7. Liver transplant on tacrolimus and elevated creatinine
    - Hold Tacrolimus until levels return
    - Can restart tacrolimus once dehydration is corrected

8. Acute cellular rejection presents as transaminitis and cholestasis
    - First 3 months post transplantation
    - Subtherapeutic tacrolimus

9. Acute portal vein clot- warfarin x 6 months

10. Major cause of death in liver transplantation is atherosclerotic cardiovascular disease #1, cancer is #2
- End stage renal disease (ESRD) occurs in 20% of patients with liver transplantation and may need kidney transplantation as well. It is tolerated great
- 10% of liver transplantation die within 1-3 months due to complications of surgery/ underlying disease

11. Post liver transplantation within a few days develops hepatic artery thrombosis, relist for liver transplantation

12. Hepatic artery thrombosis
- Major cause of graft loss and mortality
- Early (typically within 4 weeks) HAT or late HAT
- Early HAT is presents as acute, fulminant hepatic failure
- Late HAT may present with insidious, progressive cholestasis
- Hepatic artery doppler ultrasound is useful in the diagnosis
- An alternative would be CTA or MRA
- Emergent retransplantation is frequently required for early HAT in patients who present with fulminant hepatic failure
- Late-onset HAT may be managed conservatively, though outcomes are still guarded.

12. Primary graft non function is a serious and rare complication after transplantation
- 4-8% and requires retransplantation
- Clinical condition worsens within 24 hours
- Reperfusion injury
- Acute cellular rejection and hepatic artery thrombosis ruled out

13. Nine weeks after liver transplantation, biliary stricture is anastomotic and not PSC. Anastomotic biliary stricture occur ~ 8-10 weeks after liver transplantation

14. Metoclopramide increases the dose of Tacrolimus and Cyclosporine.
- Protease inhibitors for HCV may increase levels

15. Post liver transplant in Hepatitis C patient with abnormal liver enzymes
- If LFT's abnormal then liver biopsy to r/o acute rejection vs hepatitis C

16. Acute cellular rejection of liver transplantation manifested by central endotheliitis and ductulitis

- Chronic rejection is characterized by ductopenia and cholestasis

17. Commonest cancer in liver transplantation is skin cancer

18. Cirrhotic patient waiting for liver transplantation with cholecystitis - Gallbladder (GB) stent placement

Metabolic Liver diseases

1. Plasma cells have spoke wheel like appearance, diagnostic of AIH
   - Treat with prednisone

2. AIH had 90% biochemical remission in 2 weeks with treatment
   - Histological remission is 80-85% by 3 years

3. Steroids for AIH in 4 situations
   - Extreme symptoms such as fatigue
   - AST/ALT> 10 normal
   - AST/ALT > 5 n and IgG > 2N
   - Necrosis (lobular or bridging) on biopsy

4. Abnormal LFTs in patient with AIH in remission may be due to Azathioprine
   - Check metabolites
   - AIH on Azathioprine did well initially but now has possible relapse with leukopenia and abnormal liver enzymes
        - Stop Azathioprine and check metabolites
        - Possible toxicity with 6TG and 6 MMP
   - Stopping Azathioprine may cause relapse in 50-90%
   - Histology can determine response
        - If active disease, then AIH can recur
        - If no active disease, may respond better after stopping Azathioprine
   - Autoimmune hepatitis (AIH), always confirm with liver biopsy
   - May use Tacrolimus instead of Azathioprine if metabolites high

5. Liver transplantation for AIH with recurrence (15-40%)
   - Treat with corticosteroids
   - Disease activity at liver transplantation predicts recurrence
   - AIH after liver transplantation need a higher baseline level of immunosuppression

6. AIH with cirrhosis and patient wants to be pregnant on AZT
   - Check for esophageal varices and if present beta blockers or banding
   - AZT is safe and doesn't need to be stopped

7. Type 2 AIH
   - Anti-LKM 1 Antibody is positive
   - Usually presents in children
   - Associated with autoimmune thyroiditis, type 1 DM

8. Patient with elevated AMA, ASMA and transaminases, needs liver biopsy (for AIH)

8. Frailty indicates vulnerability to adverse outcomes in liver disease management

9. Liver disease + Onion skinning of bile ductules + Abnormal MRCP is PSC
   - Liver disease + Antimitochondrial Antibody = Primary biliary cholangitis (PBC)
   - Liver disease + Positive ANA = AIH

10. PBC
    - Diagnosis of PBC is 2 out of 3 - increased ALP, AMA positive, Cholangiopathy
        - If ⅔ above, then no need for liver biopsy

11. PBC associated with
    - RA
    - Sjogren's, CREST, Scleroderma
    - Hypothyroidism
    - Osteoporosis (commonest side effect)
    - Glomerulonephritis

12. PBC has increased cholesterol but NOT increased triglycerides
    - Hyperlipidemia *doesn't* increase CV risks
    - PBC has elevated IgM levels
    - Annual TSH check and q2-4 years bone densitometry test

13. PBC with mild itchiness and diffuse arthralgia in the hands - check for Rheumatoid factor

14. PBC specific antibodies besides AMA are gp210 and sp100
    - 5% antimitochondrial antibody (AMA) neg
    - *Florid ductal lesion*, large ducts infiltrated by inflammatory infiltrate, Exuberant inflammation around the bile duct, AMA positive is PBC
    - Majority are females

15. Treat PBC with URSO, calcium and vitamin D
    - Cholestyramine used for Pruritus
    - Not tolerating URSO, use Obeticholic acid
    - URSO in PBC helps reduce the risk of varices and LDL
    - URSO doesn't reduce bone disease, fatigue or pruritus

16. Young female with AMA with normal liver enzymes, no PBC now but

monitor q6-12 months

17. URSO delays progress of PBC to cirrhosis or liver transplantation
    - PBC patients often have xanthelasma, therefore check for AMA
    - Treated by URSO at 13-15 mg/kg daily. Response to URSO assessed by ALP levels
    - Obeticholic acid is farnesoid X receptor (FXR) agonist.
    - Used in combination with URSO for treatment of PBC
    - Patients with PBC are often Depressed due to fatigue. Treat depression
    - Biopsies not always needed for diagnosis of PBC (unlike AIH)
    - Elevated T Bili and INR may indicate advanced PBC and may not rectify with therapy
    - PBC may develop kidney stones

18. AIH biopsies show plasma cell portal infiltrate with interface and lobular activity
    - PBC has portal tract changes and mild lymphocytic cholangitis

19. PBC and pregnancy
    - Check serum total bile acids in first trimester to establish a baseline in the event of intrahepatic cholestasis of pregnancy

20. Treatment of overlap syndrome AIH/PBC is directed at the histological diagnosis and not clinical/ serological or biochemical parameters
    - r/o PSC
    - Overlap syndrome with mild fibrosis with biopsy showing mild portal inflammation
        - No treatment if mild
        - Azathioprine not used for induction therapy of AIH

21. Patient with increased ALP and + ANA with normal imaging and liver biopsy that shows piecemeal necrosis and plasma cells - overlap syndrome and treat the histology ie. prednisone

22. 90% of PSC also have IBD
    - Mainly UC but also CD
    - URSO is not a Rx for PSC
    - ERCP only for dominant stricture with symptoms
    - PSC is an untreatable disease that requires liver Transplantation

23. Young patient with PSC next step
    - Colonoscopy to check for UC and dysplasia
    - No need to perform liver biopsy on all patients with PSC since cholangiography is diagnostic

- Colon cancer (CRC) in 11% of PSC patients
- 30-year risk of cholangiocarcinoma is 20%
- PSC and colitis patients need colonoscopy every 1 year
- PSC without colitis patient need colonoscopy every 3-5 years

24. PSC + Liver transplantation 10 years ago
    - Increased ALP after 10 years
    - Likely diagnosis is recurrent PSC. Check MRCP

25. Overlap syndrome- Always r/o PSC

26. Liver biopsy with onion skinning is PSC. Diagnosis is through MRCP
    - Small duct PSC can have normal MRCP but typical biopsy features

27. PSC with cirrhosis develop fat soluble vitamin deficiency
    - New onset PSC with stricture, brush cytology

28. Mild abnormality of liver enzymes with cold intolerance - check TSH levels for hypothyroidism

29. Alpha 1 Antitrypsin deficiency (A1AT) disease
    - Normal phenotype is MM (normal is 75-300)
    - Reduced A1AT in PiMZ/SZ- A1AT level of 50 (mildly low) the phenotype is PiMZ
    - Severely reduced in PiZZ associated with levels of A1AT less than 40- only 1/3 develop cirrhosis
    - Most common metabolic liver disease in children
    - Most common cause of liver transplantation in children
    - A1AT deficiency is more in Caucasians
    - PAS positive globules in hepatocytes
    - A1AT is an acute phase reactant and can be falsely normal in inflammation

30. In AIAT deficiency, absence of detectable SERPINA1 protein indicates null mutation
    - Pulmonary disease without liver disease
    - Pulmonary damage is caused by unopposed action neutrophil elastase
    - Early COPD < 50 years of age

31. PiZZ mutation, excess misfolded A1AT accumulates in endoplasmic reticulum of liver cells leading to oxidative damage and fibrosis and cirrhosis

32. PAS positive reddish globules in hepatocytes
    - A1AT deficiency ZZ phenotype

- Most with the phenotype never develop disease

33. Liver biopsy showing granuloma in liver is sarcoidosis
    - May be associated with violaceous plaques or nodules over cheeks, nose and ears known as Lupus pernio

34. Sarcoidosis- liver common after lung
    - 90% no liver injury
    - Diagnosis via Liver biopsy
    - ACE level may be elevated but not specific
    - Treated with Ursodiol x 3 months. Second line is corticosteroids
    - Clinicaly significant liver injury is rare
    - 10% have progressive disease leading to cirrhosis with high ALT and AST.
    - Treatment for severe disease is Liver transplantation

35. Liver disease with hilar adenopathy is sarcoid
    - *Lupus pernio* is a common skin lesion in sarcoidosis characterized by raised patches, deep lumps, or open sores

36. CT with a central scar in the liver is FNH
    - Eovist on MRI
    - Enhancing on arterial phase on CT scan is HCC, adenomas and FNH

37. Dark pigmented bile casts- cholestasis from anabolic steroids

38. Sub centimeter suspected HCC, repeat imaging in 3-4 months since sensitivity of MRI and CT are low and more than 50% benign

39. AST> 5 x ALT check CPK for muscle injury

40. Benign recurrent intrahepatic cholestasis
    - Young patient with recurrent intermittent pruritus, jaundice and weight loss last 6 months
    - Rare FIC (bile acid transport) gene
    - Family history
    - ALP abnormal but GGT is normal, and AST/ALT is normal

41. ABCB11 gene controls bile acid export with mutations causing recurrent intrahepatic cholestasis, progressive familial intrahepatic cholestasis and intrahepatic cholestasis of pregnancy

42. Maralixibat, an ileal bile acid transport inhibitor, is the first treatment approved for Alagille's syndrome that presents with cholestasis in children

43. Gaucher's disease
   - Lysosomal storage disease
   - Accumulation of glucocerebroside in macrophages in liver spleen and bone marrow with hepatosplenomegaly
   - Inheritence is AR
   - Increased risk of HCC
   - Treatment is via Eliglustat

44. Dense liver pigmentation in Dubin-Johnson syndrome
   - Direct hyperbilirubinemia in Dubin-Johnson syndrome and Rotor syndrome
   - Indirect Hyperbilirubinemia in Gilbert syndrome and Crigler-Najjar syndrome

45. Prolonged fasting doubles T Bilirubin levels in patients with Gilbert's syndrome
   - Gilbert's syndrome due to genetic variations in UGT1A1 gene leading to decreased activity of bilirubin uridine diphosphate glucuronosyltransferase enzyme.

46. Heat stroke can cause abnormal liver enzymes
   - Heat stroke can cause liver failure

Hereditary Hemochromatosis (HH)

1. Hemochromatosis
   - Type 1 is due to HFE gene mutations
   - Type 2 (juvenile) hepcidin related
   - Type 3 (TFR related) hepcidin related
   - Type 4 hemochromatosis mutations in ferroportin, seen in african countries

2. Asymptomatic patient, phlebotomy when ferritin > 500
   - Goal is to remove 500 cc of blood per week
   - Ferritin goal of 50-100
   - Avoid Fe and vitamin C supplements
   - Phlebotomy reduces liver disease, early fibrosis, abnormal liver enzymes and liver cancer, heart disease, skin pigmentation and fatigue
      - Will not improve cirrhosis, DM, hypogonadism and arthralgias
   - Phlebotomy doesn't prevent the patient from being a blood donor

3. Liver biopsy with Ferritin > 1 k or abnormal AST/ALT
   - First degree relatives mainly screened for HH (ACG 2020)
   - No surveillance for those with fibrosis stage 3 or less
   - H63D or 65S in the absence of C282Y do not get HH
   - No further work up in patients with Fe overload without C282Y or H63D
   - Non-contrast enhanced MRI (MRIT2) to quantify hepatic iron in non-C282Y homozygote suspected HH patients
   - Liver biopsy if fibrosis or other diseases need to be ruled out
   - Phlebotomy first line of treatment in C282Y homozygote or C282Y/H63D heterozygote
   - Chelation only in case of intolerance of phlebotomy in severe anemia or heart failure. May cause renal or hepatic damage
   - Liver transplantation in HH patients with HCC or decompensated cirrhosis

4. Hereditary hemochromatosis (HH)
   - Decreased in hepcidin and failure of feedback loop
   - Juvenile hemochromatosis is deficiency of hemojuvelin
   - C282y/H63D -Complex heterozygote
      - Do not have increased iron overload and do not need phlebotomy
      - Children screened only if the wife has high iron levels
   - MRI of the liver with dark appearance indicates hemochromatosis
   - Commonest cause of death in Hereditary Hemochromatosis (HH) is HCC

5. Liver slide with Prussian blue stain for Fe but not in hepatocytes but in sinusoidal Kupffer cells- Transfusion overload

6. Prussian blue stain in HH with increased iron in hepatocytes in C282y/C282Y mutation

7. Hereditary hemochromatosis (HH) usually has Ferritin > 1000 associated with cirrhosis

8. H63D homozygosity doesn't cause hemochromatosis
   - If patient has children check the spouse for C282Y to evaluate for compound heterozygous HH
   - If husband is homozygous for C282Y gene, then check wife for HH gene

9. Oral iron chelating agents such as deferasirox used in secondary iron overload

10. HH may be associated with pseudogout

Wilson's Disease (WD)

1. Young patient with mental status change with jaundice, minor tremors, T Bili increased, INR increased
   - AST>ALT
   - ALP:T Bili <4
   - Age alone should not be the basis for eliminating WD
   - WD possible in any individual with liver abnormalities of uncertain cause

2. Wilson's disease with fulminant liver failure
   - Treatment is liver transplantation
   - Asterixis is a sign of fulminant liver failure
   - Acute Liver Failure with nonimmune hemolytic anemia including acute intravascular hemolysis needs urgent evaluation for transplantation

3. Autosomal recessive disorder with ATP7B gene mutation
   - Genetic test for ATP7B screens first-degree relatives of proband
   - First-degree relatives of newly diagnosed WD must be screened
   - Within a pedigree with WD, anybody with signs or symptoms of WD, should be evaluated regardless of closeness

4. Wilson's disease suspected but with negative ceruloplasmin and urinary copper, next step is liver biopsy with Cu staining

5. Wilson's disease has
   - Decreased uric acid
   - Recurrent self-limited nonimmune hemolysis
   - Unexplained liver disease+ neurological or psychiatric disorder.
   - May involve renal, musculoskeletal, cardiac, or endocrine
   - Extremely low ceruloplasmin(<5 mg/dl) strongly suggests a WD
      - Normal ceruloplasmin does not exclude WD
   - Basal 24-h urinary excretion of copper >100 µg/24-h in symptomatic patients
      - 40 µg/24h may indicate WD in asymptomatic individuals or children and needs further investigation.
   - Hepatic parenchymal copper content >250 µg/g occurs in WD
      - Normal hepatic copper (<50 µg/g dry weight) excludes WD
   - Diagnostic scoring systems useful in diagnosing or refuting WD
   - Prognostic scoring systems may be helpful with therapy

6. Definitive diagnosis of WD is presence of Kaiser-Fleisher rings on eye examination, low ceruloplasmin, increased 24-hour total urine copper
   - Ceruloplasmin has low positive predictive value

- Urinary 24 hours TOTAL copper. Significant if > 100mcg/ 24 hours
- 50% have Kayser-Fleischer (KF) rings
    - With neurological findings 90-95% have KF rings
- Histology is nonspecific
    - Mallory bodies
    - Steatosis
    - Chronic hepatitis
    - Glycogen vacuolation of nucleus
- In a patient with Kayser-Fleischer ring on regular examination, no need for slit lamp examination

7. All WD should be initiated on lifelong medical therapy
    - Initial treatment is a chelating agent such as D- penicillamine or trientine (better tolerated).
    - Aymptomatic patients can be treated with chelating agent / Zn
    - Transition to maintenance therapy depends on time on therapy > than 1 year and clinical and biochemical response
    - Maintenance therapy may be a lower dose chelating agent (D-penicillamine or trientine) or full-dose zinc
    - Avoid intake of foods and water containing high concentrations of copper during the first year of treatment

8. Patients on chelation therapy require a CBC and urinalysis for duration of therapy
    - Yearly 24-h urinary copper while on medication, or in patients on chelating agents after a temporary period (48 h) off drug, should be measured

9. Overtreatment may be indicated by development of cytopenias or retention of tissue iron associated with raised serum ferritin
    - Confirmed by a low serum Cu and a very low 24-h urinary Cu
    - 24-h urinary Cu excretion is disproportionately low for the dose of chelator specifically <100 µg/24- h
    - For Zn therapy, 24-h urinary copper <20 µg/24-h suggests overtreatment.

10. After liver transplantation, medical treatment for WD is unnecessary
    - WD and severe unresponsive hepatic disease
    - Advancedliver disease who fail to tolerate medical therapy
    - ALF
    - Acute liver injury require early transplant referral
    - Liver failure and HCC

11. WD with cirrhosis need HCC screening and surveillance

12. Treatment for WD should be continued during pregnancy
   - D- Penicillamine has known teratogenic potential
   - Chelation therapy at a reduced dosage with monitoring of liver function each trimester is another option.
   - Zinc is safe; if a prospective mother is switched to Zn, clinical stability on Zn should be established before the pregnancy
   - Breastfeeding while on therapy entails potential harms to the infant-risk benefits should be individualized.

13. Effective treatment may lead to improved neurological and psychiatric features
   - May alleviate symptoms of neurologic WD, including parkinsonism, dystonia, and chorea
   - Persisting or severe psychiatric features may benefit from psychotropic medications or counseling.

14. Wilson's disease patient may present with
   - Jaundice and fatigue
   -AST>ALT
   - Alkaline phosphatase is low compared to other liver enzymes
   - Reduced Hct and increased indirect hyperbilirubinemia
   - On SSRI for depression or psychiatric issues
   - If liver tissue is already available, most definitive test for Wilson's disease is hepatic liver concentration

NAFLD/NASH

1. In NAFLD without fibrosis, CAD is a complication. Treat with statins

2. A liver biopsy should be performed in NAFLD patients who are at risk for significant fibrosis
   - DM
   - Increasing age (older than 50)
   - BMI greater than 28
   - Increased serum AST/ALT ratio (greater than 0.8)
   - Low platelet count
   - Mitochondrial disease
   - Iron overload

3. Commonest cause of death in NASH is cardiovascular disease

4. Bariatric surgery reduces NASH

5. NALFD with refractory ascites undergoes TIPPS, still has ascites, fever, pain. Check US for occluded TIPPS. Needs paracentesis to rule out infection prior to TIPS revision

6. Liver biopsy with fatty liver cells is NASH
   - Hypertriglyceridemia is a risk
   - Amiodarone can cause NASH
   - Weight loss can cause reversal of NASH but not predictable
   - NASH can occur after liver transplantation

7. Liver cells with microvesicular fat within
   - AFLP
   - Reye's syndrome
   - HAART
   - Tetracycline and massive aspirin use
   - Valproic acid

8. Lean NAFLD diagnosed in individuals with NAFLD(AGA 2022)
   - BMI <25 kg/m2 (non-Asian race) or BMI <23 kg/m2 (Asian race)
   - Evaluated routinely for type 2 diabetes mellitus, dyslipidemia and hypertension
   - Risk stratified for hepatic fibrosis to identify advanced fibrosis or cirrhosis.

9. Screening for lean NAFLD in individuals > 40 years with type 2 diabetes mellitus.

- NAFLD in lean individuals with metabolic diseases (DM2, dyslipidemia and hypertension), elevated liver enzymes or incidentally noted hepatic steatosis
- No NAFLD screening for lean individuals in the general population

10. Fatty liver in lean individuals
   - HIV
   - Lipodystrophy
   - Lysosomal acid lipase deficiency
   - Familial hypobetalipoproteinemia
   - Medication-induced hepatic steatosis (methotrexate, amiodarone, tamoxifen and steroids)

11. Liver biopsy only if there is uncertainty regarding causes of liver injury and/or the stage of liver fibrosis

12. Serum indices (NAFLD fibrosis score and Fibrosis-4 score) and imaging techniques (transient elastography and magnetic resonance elastography) are alternatives to liver biopsy for fibrosis staging

13. Lifestyle intervention, including exercise, diet modification and avoidance of fructose- and sugar-sweetened drinks, to target a modest weight loss of 3%–5% is suggested
   - Vitamin E in lean persons with biopsy-confirmed nonalcoholic steatohepatitis, but without type 2 diabetes mellitus or cirrhosis
   - Pioglitazone 30 mg daily in people without cirrhosis
   - The role of glucagon-like peptide-1 agonists and sodium-glucose cotransporter-2 inhibitors in lean NAFLD is not defined

14. HCC surveillance with abdominal ultrasound with or without serum α-fetoprotein twice per year in lean NAFLD with cirrhosis.

15. Hyperlipidemia from cholestatic disease does not increase risk of atherosclerosis
   - Cholestatic liver disease may cause fat soluble vitamin deficiency

16. Vit E showed histologic improvement in NASH without improvement in liver fibrosis
   - Obitocholic acid improves histology and fibrosis score in NASH

17. NASH with 2-4 fibrosis at increased risk of liver related morbidity and events

18. Rate of progression depends on baseline severity, genetics, comorbidities and environment

19. Cardiovascular disease and non-hepatic malignancy are most common cause of death in NASH without advanced fibrosis

20. Liver disease is the commonest cause of death in NASH with advanced fibrosis

21. Insulin resistance and systemic inflammation leads to NASH disease progression

22. Statins are safe in compensated cirrhosis. Statins with careful monitoring in high risk cardiovascular disease in decompensated cirrhosis

23. Hypertriglyceridemia managed by omega-3 fatty acids, icosapent ethyl, or fibrates

24. DM2 are a higher risk of NASH with advanced disease and need to be screened for fibrosis
   - NASH should be screened for DM2
   - NASH with fibrosis > 1 should avoid alcohol completely
   - NASH more common in men with androgen deficiency but no routine checking of testosterone level

25. Androgen excess can worsen insulin resistance in women with PCOS and contribute to NASH

26. No screening of general population for NASH

27. FIB-4 in patients with hepatic steatosis or suspected NASH based on metabolic risk factors

28. Screen for advanced fibrosis in patients with
   - DM2
   - Medically complicated obesity
   - Fhx of cirrhosis
   - Significant alcohol consumption

29. FIB-4 initially and every 1-2 years in patients with pre-DM, DM2

30. Aminotransferases can be normal in advanced NASH

31. First degree relatives of patients with NASH cirrhosis should undergo counseling regarding risks and screening for liver disease with advanced

fibrosis

32. Controlled attenuation parameter (CAP) can identify steatosis.
    - MRI-PDFF (proton density fat fraction) can quantify steatosis
    - MRI- PDFF has the highest sensitivity to assess liver fat
    - If FIB-4 >/= 1.3 VCTE (Vibration controlled elastography)
    - MRE (magnetic resonance elastography) and ELF (Enhanced liver fibrosis)can used to evaluate for advanced fibrosis

33. Management with caloric deficit diet with more fiber + unsaturated fat and less saturated fats or calories
    - Increased activity levels and prescriptive exercises have benefits in NASH independent of weight loss
    - Bariatric surgery is a therapeutic options in patient with compensated cirrhosis and leads to reduction in cardiovascular and cancer mortality

34. Semaglutide can be considered for its approved indications in DM2/ Obesity as it improves NASH and cardiovascular mortality

35. Pioglitazone improves NASH and can be considered for patients with NASH in the context of patients with DM2

36. Vitamin E can be considered in some select individuals without DM2 as it improves NASH

37. Semaglutide, pioglitazone, and vitamin E do not demonstrate antifibrotic benefit

38. Metformin, ursodeoxycholic acid, dipeptidyl peptidase-4, statins, and silymarin are well studied in NASH and should not be used as a treatment for NASH

39. Improvement in ALT or reduction in liver fat content by imaging can be used as a surrogate for histological improvement in disease activity.

Hepatitis, Infectious

1. HBV vaccine
   - Travelers to Asia, Pacific islands
   - Travelers to Africa
   - Travelers to eastern Europe
   - Non-monogamous

2. Patients with Hepatitis BsAb+ that is protective against Hepatitis B while being started on Rituximab need to take antiviral prophylaxis during the treatment and 12 -18 months after completing chemotherapy

3. Risk of HBV reactivation when HCV is treated
   - Check HbsAg, HBeAg and HBV DNA, if +
      - Check HBcAb and HBeAb
   - If HBcAb is + but HBV DNA neg or HbsAg neg then check monthly
   - If HBsAg +, HBV DNA+, then HBV prophylaxis
   - If HBsAb + then protected and no check ups

4. Treat with HBV immunoglobulin after needle stick
   - Not spread through breast milk

5. Treat HBV if ALT is 2 x normal or HBV DNA is > 20k

6. Hepatitis BeAg neg chronic active Hepatitis B need to be on lifelong treatment - may get a drug holiday but disease can come back after stopping medications

7. HBV coinfection with HIV
   - Increased chronic HBV
   - Increased HBV viral load
   - More rapid progression to cirrhosis
   - Increase in liver related mortality

8. Intravenous drug users with ascites and HBV
   - CT scan shows non-visualization of hepatic veins likely have BCS
      - Anticoagulants and diuretics/ TIPS
   - Western BCS by thrombosis of hepatic vein. Asia/ Africa due to IVC membrane

9. Young female with HBV and in third trimester and HCV
   - Treat only if HBV> 200K

- Tenofovir/Telbivudine in 3rd trimester
- If HBV < 200k then child gets vaccine + IVIg within 12 hours
- HCV treatment 3 months after birth

10. Teenager with HBsAg+ and HBeAg+ normal ALT and DNA > 5 million.
   - Biopsies with scant inflammation
   - Immune tolerant HBV
   - Treatment is conservative

11. High dose HBV vaccine to patients on hemodialysis and HIV

12. Treatment not indicated in HBV if liver tests are normal, HBV DNA < 2k and HBV e ag neg

13. Inactive HBV patient who presents with increased LFTs with increased HBV DNA with IgM HBc Ab+ with HDV/HCV negative is reactivation of HBV

14. Decompensated cirrhosis and chronic HBV treated with antiviral regardless of HBV DNA levels

15. Patient with no response to HBV vaccine - check for HbsAg

16. Patient with HBV and HCV show rapid progression to cirrhosis

17. Highest HBV infection is sub-Saharan Africa

18. HBV treated with PO antiviral agent until
   - HBV DNA undetectable
   - LFTs normal
   - HBsAg+, HBeAg-, HBeAb+
   - Possibly stop in 6 months after seroconversion
   - However, HBeAg neg HBV cannot stop antivirals

19. Acute HBV managed by observation unless there is acute liver failure or protracted severe disease
   - Acute Hepatitis B stable, discharge for outpatient follow up

20. HBV with encephalopathy and increased INR
   - Fulminant HBV with liver failure
   - 1/3 are already positive with HBsAb
   - 1/4th already lose HBeAg

21. HBV disease responsive to entecavir, stop in 6 months if no precore

mutant or liver transplant

22. Hepatitis B vaccine response
    - Better if IM than SQ
    - Less in immunocompromised

23. HBV improved for 2-4 weeks and then worsened with liver failure, check for HDV
    - Check for HDV also in patients with hepatitis B with HIV, drug use, risk of STD, and abnormal liver enzymes with low HBV count
    - 20-25% of HBV/HDV coinfection have fulminant liver failure

24. HBV/HDV coinfection need HCC screening/ surveillance

25. Treatment of HDV is interferon x 12 months

26. Hepatitis D treated with interferon. No sustained viral remission
    - Asymptomatic carrier, check liver enzymes q 6 months

27. Direct acting antiviral therapy (DAAT) for HCV with sudden increase in liver enzymes with undetected HCV RNA, Check for Hep B

28. HBV DNA > 2 k with elevated liver enzymes and neg Hepatitis Be Ag, treat with Tenofovir now and long term

29. HBV DNA > 20K with elevated liver enzymes (ALT> 2N) and positive hepatitis Be Ag treated with antivirals

30. If HBcAb+ but HBeAg and HBeAb negative, then no Hepatitis B since HBcAb is false positive
    - Healthy carrier with normal liver enzymes, HBsAg neg, HBcAb + and HBsAb neg doesn't have HBV

31. Hep B pregnant patient
    - First trimester with < 24 k DNA and normal liver enzymes
    - Recheck in 3rd trimester
    - HBV DNA> 200k with increased risk of infection of child
    - Treat HBV at any time if there is an indication
    - *Tenofovir disoproxil fumarate* is preferred
    - Mainstay of preventing mother to child transmission of HBV is HBV vaccination of the infant

32. Tenofovir alafenamide (TAF) for Hepatitis B has better renal and bone

disease profile

33. HCV with HBcAb+
    - DAAT for HCV
    - Recheck HBV at end of treatment and in 3 months after treatment

34. HBeAg neg HBV pregnant female with HBV DNA < 200k but > 2000 with abnormal liver enzymes
    - Treat after delivery and breastfeeding

35. The AGA suggests against using anti-HBs Ab status to guide antiviral prophylaxis for all risk groups.
    - Entecavir over lamivudine for prophylaxis

36. Antiviral prophylaxis for HBV in high-risk patients
    - AntiHBcAb+ patients treated with B cell–depleting agents (such as rituximab, ofatumumab) continued for 12 months after completion of therapy
    - HBsAg+/anti-HBc+ patients treated with anthracycline derivatives (doxorubicin), moderate-dose (10–20 mg prednisone daily or equivalent) or high-dose (>20 mg prednisone daily or equivalent) corticosteroids daily for ≥4 weeks. Continued for 6 months after completion

37. Antiviral prophylaxis for hepatitis B patients in moderate risk patients. Continue prophylaxis for 6 months after completion
    - Anti-HBc+ patients treated with
        - anti-TNF
        - Other cytokine or integrin inhibitors (for example, abatacept, ustekinumab, natalizumab, vedolizumab)
        - Tyrosine kinase inhibitors (for example, imatinib, nilotinib)
        - Moderate dose or high dose prednisone
        - Anthracycline derivatives (such as doxorubicin, epirubicin).
    - HBsAg+/anti-HBc+ patients treated with low-dose (<10 mg prednisone daily or equivalent) corticosteroids for duration of ≥4 weeks

38. While on TNF-inhibitors in patient with HBsAb + patient, monitor ALT and HBV DNA tests q 3 months

39. Immunotolerant Hepatitis B managed by serial liver enzymes
    - Immune controlled Hepatitis B i.e., inactive carrier state in African patient needs HCC surveillance after age of 20 years
    - Hep B with decompensated cirrhosis with any detectable virus treated by entecavir or tenofovir

40. Hepatitis A associated with child day care centers

41. Relapsing hepatitis A occurs a few weeks after apparent recovery
    - Arthralgias
    - Rash

42. Acute Hepatitis A virus (HAV) may have a relapsing and cholestatic form
    - HAV vaccine and immunoglobulins for contacts
    - HAV IgG only for immunocompromised

43. Patient with prolonged cholestatic jaundice after visiting Africa
    - Cholestatic hepatitis A with prolonged jaundice and pruritus

44. Acute Hepatitis A, continue to monitor and treat. Household contacts treated with IgG to protect from current exposure

45. Patients with chronic liver disease should receive 1 dose of HAV vaccination with 1 dose of immunoglobulin as preexposure prophylaxis

46. Hepatitis E virus
    - Pig farm in Midwest
    - Eating raw pork or deer meat associated with Hepatitis E
    - 20% have antiHEV antibody in the US
    - Self-limited in immunocompetent
    - Does not spread in households
    - Treatment is ribavirin for 12 weeks
    - PEG interferon may also be effective

47. HEV infection in solid organ transplantation
    - Consider reduction of immunosupression
    - If still detectable then Ribavarin

48. s/p Liver transplantation with CMV of the liver
    - Fever, leukopenia, systemic symptoms
    - Within 6 months of liver tx
    - CMV + donor/ CMV neg recipient
    - Preemptive therapy of CMV prevents
    - Test for CMV PCR

49. Post transplantation CMV
    - Commonest infection
    - 3-12 months after transplantation
    - Usually after antibody treatment
    - Presents with leukopenia, systemic symptoms, abdominal pain, n/v and

abnormal liver enzymes

50. Echinococcal cyst
    - Comes from dog feces (not sheep)
    - Treat with PO albendazole and percutaneous drainage
    - Eosinophilia, diagnosed through ELISA

51. Amoebic liver abscess
    - 10 x more in men
    - Hepatic abscess in less than 1% of intestinal infection
    - Protozoa present in 40% of stool microscopy
    - Abscess positive for organism in < 20%

52. BCG vaccine can rarely cause mycobacterium bovis infection of liver

53. Herpetic encephalitis in older individuals with normal T Bili but AST/ALT >1000, confused, temporal lobe involvement in brain. Treat with acyclovir and low threshold transplantation

Hepatitis C (HCV)

1. Antibodies to hepatitis C detectable only after 8 weeks if exposure

2. HCV infection
   - 15-30% have no risk factors.
   - Present in 80% of IVDU
   - Genotype 1 is most common in Americas and Europe

3. Simplified HCV therapy
   - Adults with chronic HCV (any genotype) who do not have cirrhosis
   - No previous HCV treatment

4. Sofosbuvir should not be coadministered with amiodarone
   - Treatment of 1 a HCV on amiodarone is glecaprevir/ pibrentasvir x 12 weeks

5. Direct acting antiviral (DAA):
   - 1. Protease inhibitors that end in 'previr'
   - 2. Polymerase inhibitors
       - Nucleoside inhibitors
           - NS5a such as velpatasvir and Pibrentasvir
           - NS5b inhibitors such as sofosbuvir
       - Non-nucleoside inhibitors
   - Decompensated cirrhosis, do NOT treat with a protease inhibitor (no previr)
   - If anemia, then no Ribavirin

6. Hepatitis C therapy of treatment naive without cirrhosis
   - Glecaprevir/pibrentasvir x 8 weeks - all genotypes
   - Sofosbuvir/ velpatasvir x 12 weeks- all genotypes
   - Sofosbuvir/ledipasvir x 12 week - 1,4-6

7. Hepatitis C treatment of compensated cirrhosis
   - Glecaprevir/pibrentasvir x 8 weeks (12 weeks for HIV coinfection)
   - Sofosbuvir/velpatasvir x 12 weeks
   - Sofosbuvir/ledipasvir x 12 weeks for 1, 4-6

8. Hepatitis C therapy for DAA failure (sofosbuvir based failure)
   - Sofosbuvir/velpatasvir/voxilaprevir x 12 weeks (genotype 3- add Ribavarin)
   - Glecaprevir/pibrentasvir x 16 weeks (not recommended genotype 3 sofosbuvir/NS5A experienced patients and failure of NS3 or 4 protease

inhibitors/DAA combo)

9. Hepatitis C therapy of DAA failure (Elbasvir/Grazoprevir)
   - Sofosbuvir/ velpatasvir/ voxilaprevir x 12 weeks (genotype 3- add Ribavarin)

10. Hepatitis C therapy of DAA failure (Glecaprevir/pibrentasvir)
    - Glecaprevir/pibrentasvir + Daily sofosbuvir and ribavarin x 16 weeks
    - Sofosbuvir/ velpatasvir/voxilaprevir x 12 weeks (Ribavarin in compensated cirrhosis)

11. Multiple DAA treatment failures
    - Sofosbuvir/velpatasvir/voxilaprevir + ribavarin x 24 weeks
    - Glecaprevir/pibrentasvir + Sofosbuvir and ribavarin x 16 weeks (24 weeks if genotype 3 with cirrhosis)

12. Hepatitis C therapy with Decompensated cirrhosis (Ribavirin eligible)
    - Sofosbuvir/velpatasvir/ ribavarin weight based x 12 weeks
    - Sofosbuvir/ledipasvir + low dose ribavarin x 12 weeks for 1, 4-6

13. Hepatitis C therapy with Decompensated cirrhosis (Ribavarin ineligible)
    - Sofosbuvir/velpatasvir x 24 weeks
    - Sofosbuvir/ledipasvir x 24 weeks for genotypes 1, 4-6

14. Hepatitis C therapy in prior treatment failure with sofobuvir or NS5A inhibitor
    - Sofosbuvir/velpatasvir + ribavirin x 24 weeks
    - Sofosbuvir/ledipasvir + low dose initial ribavirin x 24 weeks

15. Post treatment assessment of cure of HCV
    - Quantitative HCV RNA and a hepatic function panel at 12 weeks
    - Evaluate for other causes of liver disease with elevated transaminase levels after achieving SVR.

16. Patients in whom initial HCV treatment fails to achieve cure (SVR)
    - Should be evaluated for retreatment by a specialist
    - Check hepatic function panel, CBC and INR every 6 to 12 months
    - Advise patients to avoid excess alcohol use.
    - Acute HCV rarely causes severe acute hepatitis

17. Children with HCV
    - Sofosbuvir/ledipasvir approved > 3 years of age
    - Sofosbuvir/velpatasvir > 6 years
    - Glecaprevir/pibrentasvir > 12 years

18. No antiviral therapy for pregnant women with HCV or while breastfeeding
- Invasive monitoring avoided to reduce the risk of transmission to the child

19. *Hepatitis patient with severe hepatitis, negative virology and pending serology Likely to have AIH*

20. Porphyria cutanea tarda (PCT) skin lesions indicates HCV

21. Patient with HCV and HBV
- Risk of HBV reactivation
- All HCV patients tested for HBV
- Prophylaxis of HBV only if inactive HBV
- Treatment of HBV if active HBV
- If anti-HBsAb + no further evaluation
- Patients with anti-HBcAb but not HBsAb, check monthly after completing DAA
- DAAT for hepatitis C with sudden increase in liver enzymes with undetected HCV RNA, CHECK FOR Hep B

22. Patient coinfected with HBV and HCV with + sAg and evidence of active replication
- Treat with HBV therapy during treatment of HCV and for 12 weeks after therapy with close monitoring

23. HCV coinfection with HIV or hepatitis B increases risk of fibrosis

24. Patient with ascites and HCV with elevated AFP with Portal Vein clot and negative MRI
- AFP > 220 is specific for HCC
- MRI not sensitive in the presence of ascites
- Triple phase CT to r/o HCC next

25. Hepatitis C with low levels of autoimmune markers such as ANA, Rheumatoid factor, Antithyroid antibody etc. is still only HCV
- May cause cryoglobulinemia

26. HCV with discrepancy between the elastography and FibroSure blood test, patient needs liver biopsy

27. Mavyret (Glecaprevir/Pibrentasvir) for renal failure

28. After HCV SVR, recurrence is < 1%, fibrosis slows, and cirrhosis may improve

29. Factors that predispose clearance of HCV
   - Jaundice, symptomatic
   - Females
   - Children
   - Absence of HIV and schistosomiasis

30. HCV vertical transmission
   - Sexual transmission of HCV is < 0.1%
   - No treatment for HCV vertical transmission
   - 4-10% vertical transmission
   - HCV in pregnant women, risk to the baby is 5%. 10% if HIV +
   - Check HBV and HIV

31. 20% of non-Hodgkin's B cell lymphoma is HCV
   - Porphyria cutanea tarda (PCT) HCV in 90%
   - NHL and autoimmune ITP are also associated with HCV
   - Porphyria cutanea tarda (PCT) with HCV, check for Urine porphyrins and not cryoglobulins

32. Needlestick with + HCV RNA and acute hepatitis
   - Repeat RNA in 3-4 months
   - Clears spontaneously when symptomatic

33. Hepatitis C patients do not automatically check for HBV. Check HBV in the following:
   - Immigrants from High prevalence areas
   - HIV+
   - Homosexuals
   - Intravenous drug use
   - Children born to parents from high prevalence area

34. HCV with decompensated cirrhosis with moderate to severe hepatic impairment following therapy is not recommended
   - Any protease inhibitor-containing regimen (eg, glecaprevir, grazoprevir, and voxilaprevir).
   - Interferon regimen

35. Hepatitis C hemodialysis for kidney transplant evaluation
   - Determine if patient is consented for HCV + donor

- Can be successfully treated after kidney transplantation

36. Recipients of organ transplant from HCV donors should be treated for hepatitis C immediately in the perioperative period

37. 30% of HCV clear up on their own. 70% chronic
    - Following 8–12-week therapy, recheck viral load in 3 months followed by 6-12 months

38. HCV with SVR - HCC risks remain

39. Pregnant patient has HCV with HBeAg + with DNA ~ 30 k. Treat HCV 3 months after birth

40. HCV with cryoglobulinemia (Essential mixed cryoglobulinemia)
    - If mild treat with Hepatitis C treatment
        - Regimen approved for renal issues in Heptatitis C is elbasvir/ grazoprevir
    - Skin shows purpura
    - Elevated cryoglobulins, low complements, renal disease
    - If severe symptoms with renal failure and glomerulonephritis, treat with plasmapheresis, rituximab and corticosteroids. HCV treatment afterwards

41. Acute HCV
    - Treat with antivirals (just like chronic HCV)
    - Many of these are cured specially IL28B genotype CC> TT or CT

42. Fibrosing acute cholestatic HCV
    - HCV load is very high
    - Chronic HCV associated with immunosuppression
    - Rapidly progressive cholestatic hepatitis
    - Diagnosis through histology
    - Rx by directing acting antiviral therapy

43. In HCV and chronic kidney disease
    - No dose adjustment in direct-acting antivirals is required when using recommended regimens

7. BILE DUCT AND PANCREAS

Bile duct and Gallstones

1. Gallstone formation
   - Cholesterol supersaturation
   - Reduced GB contraction
   - Increase nucleation
   - Increased mucin

2. Cholesterol stones
   - 50 yo Caucasians
   - 30 yo Pima Indians
   - Octreotide, estrogens, ceftriaxone and clofibrate cause gallstones
   - Parity
   - Obesity
   - Rapid weight loss
   - Patients on TPN

3. Black pigment stones
   - Females
   - Cirrhosis
   - Chronic hemolysis (Hemolytic anemias)
   - Ileal disease
   - Hyperbilirubinemia
   - Mechanical valve
   - Old age> 70
   - Hemolysis such as sickle cell anemia, cirrhosis and PSC
   - Cystic fibrosis
   - TPN
   - Gilbert's syndrome

4. Brown stones with CBD strictures and recurrent pyogenic cholangitis

5. Biliary colic > 70% of second attack within 2 years
   - Interferes with daily activity, often seeking medical attention such as ER or urgent care
   - Resolves completely between attacks
   - GB pain is nocturnal and not always associated with fatty foods
   - People with DM not at a higher risk

6. Patient with gallstones but doesn't have typical biliary colic is likely not related to the gallstones

7. Cholangitis presents with elevated T Bili with increased temperature with

pain
- Treat by going directly to ERCP
- Aspirin/ NSAIDS are not a contraindication to sphincterotomy
- ERCP within 48 hours (ASGE 2021)
- Biliary drainage + sphincterotomy stone removal better than stent alone

8. Elevated T bili > 4 and dilated CBD >10 mm indicative of CBD stone

9. Charcots triad of cholangitis is fever, jaundice, right upper quadrant pain
- Reynauds pentad is Charcot's triad along with confusion and hypotension

10. Increased risk of bleeding with sphincterotomy in cholangitis
- Ductal clearance in cholangitis is associated with shorter hospital stay, earlier clinical improvement and less procedures

11. Gallstones associated with Right colon cancer
- Cholecystectomy not associated with colon cancer

12. Bouveret's syndrome is cholecystoduodenal fistula due to fistulization of a large gallstone from the gallbladder into the duodenal bulb
- May cause gallstone ileus
- Gastric outlet obstruction

13. Acute cholecystitis more severe in men
- Develops in 20% of biliary colic
- On HIDA, acute cholecystitis if no filling of GB after 60 min
- If a patient with acute cholecystitis is not a candidate for surgery or percutaneous cholecystostomy then lumen apposing metal stent (LAMS) placement

14. *Gallstone pancreatitis*
- *Cholecystectomy during hospitalization*
- In non-surgical candidates ERCP with sphincterotomy

15. Gallstone pancreatitis is associated with larger cystic duct, numerous GB stones and smaller size of the gallstones

16. Large choledocholithiasis large balloon dilation after sphincterotomy better than endoscopic sphincterotomy alone (ASGE 2019)

17. ALP, AST, ALT in the 1000's is consistent with CBD stone

18. Roux en y gastric bypass with CBD stone needs balloon assisted ERCP

19. Patient with acute pancreatitis
- AST/ALT is 3 x normal is highly predictive of gallstones. 50% of patients with gallstone pancreatitis have increased liver enzymes
- Acute liver enzyme elevation in pancreatitis is specific but not very sensitive for biliary source
- ERCP for sepsis/Cholangitis and acute pancreatitis

20. Gallstone dissolution with URSO is 20% after 2 years with 50% chance of recurrence. Works better on smaller stones and increased cholesterol content (floating stones)

21. ERCP for elective CBD stones on DAPT x 12 months- Schedule/ delay ERCP until after the minimal length of treatment completed
- Moderate risk of CBD stones, evaluate first with MRCP or EUS

22. Gallstones in pregnancy due to
- Increased progesterone with reduced GB emptying and increased GB volume
- Increased cholesterol saturation

23. Pregnant women with biliary colic should undergo lap cholecystectomy in 2nd trimester to reduce risk of C section

24. Acalculus cholecystitis occurs in critical illnesses, burns, infections etc and presents with fever and hyperamylasemia
- Treated by surgery if it can be tolerated vs percutaneous cholecystostomy

25. Emphysematous cholecystitis occurs in diabetics and elderly
- May occur without gallstones
- Prompt antibiotics, surgery or percutaneous cholecystostomy

26. Recurrent pyogenic cholangitis:
- Common in far east
- Clonorchis sinensis or Ascaris
- Primary intrahepatic stones and recurrent cholangitis
- Brown pigment stones
- Increases risk of cholangiocarcinoma

27. Recurrent pyogenic cholangitis managed by resection if the affected liver lobe is atrophied or has cholangiocarcinoma

28. Be familiar with image of Mirrizi's syndrome which is compression of

CHD and increasing LFT's/ jaundice due to stone lodged in the cystic duct or GB neck

29. Microlithiasis of gallbladder/ bile duct
   - No treatment recommended after first episode of pancreatitis.
   - Treat only after the second episode

30. Young patient with post cholecystectomy pain
   - Trial of tricyclics for visceral hyperalgesia

31. Short term TPN use with jaundice
   - Cholestasis after TPN x 8 weeks, check for gallstones
   - Progressive liver disease associated with TPN occurs only after 6 months to several years of being on TPN
      - Managed by switching to a fish oil lipid formulation

32. Asymptomatic patient s/p cholecystectomy with isolated change in intrahepatic duct caliber found incidentally is due to surgical damage and needs non-invasive testing such as MRCP
   - Focally dilated right liver lobe bile ducts indicates possible intraoperative injury during cholecystectomy

33. Cystic duct leak- 10 Fr. biliary stent
   - CBD transection, Bilateral PTC followed by hepaticojejunostomy
   - Peripheral intrahepatic bile duct leak, place plastic biliary stent

34. Bile leak with biloma
   - First step is to drain the biloma

35. Complicated cholecystectomy and few months later with CBD stricture
   - Treat with stent placement
   - Works in 80%

36. Intraoperative hepatic artery injury during cholecystectomy
   - Patient with RUQ pain
   - CT scan showed shrunken left liver lobe
   - History of Cholecystectomy (CCx)
   - Normal AST and ALT
   - Elevated ALP and GGT

37. Young patient with reduced HIDA GB ejection fraction (EF) and dyspepsia
   - Cholecystectomy can be performed although may not resolve symptoms
   - 12% of asymptomatic patients have low GB EF

38. Bile duct lining with rounded cryptosporidium seen in AIDS cholangiopathy with really low CD4 count and treated with nitazoxanide

39. HIV cholangiopathy- papillary stenosis and irregular bile ducts associated with low CD4 count

40. In Salmonella typhi carriers, permissive niche is usually biliary tract and the gallbladder
    - Cholecystectomy eliminates carrier state for typhoid
    - Asymptomatic salmonella carriers have higher risk of gb cancer

41. Ascaris in the biliary tree
    - Common in south east US in pig farmers
    - Cholangitis and pancreatitis
    - Mild pulmonary symptoms are common
    - Ascaris lumbricoides and Opisthorchis sinensis cause recurrent pyogenic cholangitis
    - Diagnosed with eggs in stool
    - Treated with Albendazole, Ivermectin or Mebendazole. ERCP with sphincterotomy and balloon sweep

42. Congenital anomalies of GB include
    - Wandering GB with a long mesentery
    - Micro GB associated with cystic fibrosis
    - Septated hourglass GB
    - Phrygian cap with inverted fundus

43. Type 1 choledochal cyst with abnormal pancreaticobiliary junction with long common channel, treatment is surgery to prevent cholangiocarcinoma
    - Treated with Roux-n-Y hepaticojejunostomy
    - Cancer risk is highest with type 1 and Type 4 choledochal cyst

44. Choledochocele is treated with ERCP sphincterotomy
    - Caroli's disease presents < 30 years with cholangitis or non-cirrhotic portal hypertension and variceal bleeding

45. Anomalous pancreaticobiliary junction
    - Increase risk of stones and pancreatitis
    - Associated with biliary cysts
    - Risk for gb cancer and biliary cyst cancer
    - Union of cbd and pd outside the duodenal wall >8 mm
    - Increase in amylase in bile duct > 8k

46. Anomalous pancreaticobiliary junction

- Kimura Type BP- bile duct joins the PD
- Kimura type PB- PD joins the CBD, associated with pancreatitis
- Kimura long Y type- long common channel
- Treated with pancreatic sphincterotomy and stent placement
- May need cholecystectomy to reduce the risk of GB cancer

47. Portal biliopathy
- Extrinsic compression of bile duct from engorged veins due to portal vein thrombosis and cavernous transformation
- Treated by TIPS

48. In a dilated CBD MRI is UNLIKELY to add to a good CT in looking for tumors

49. Duodenal perforations during ERCP is 3 in 1000
- Type 1 - lateral or medial duodenal wall due to shaft of endoscope needing surgery
- Type 2 related to sphincterotomy- non surgical treatment with covered metal stent
- Type 3 - Guidewire related perforation- non surgical
- Type 4- only retroperitoneal air noted due to air insufflation or miniscule rupture and management is non-surgical

50. PSC treated by ERCP with balloon dilation of dominant strictures

51. Large duct PSC surveillance for cholangiocarcinoma
- Cross sectional imaging and CA 19-9 q 6-12 months
- Small ducts PSC and < 20 years - No surveillance
- Surveillance only after age 20 years
- Cholangiocarcinoma is independent of duration of PSC or IBD
    - 10-15% of PSC (20% in 30 years)
- Increase in GB cancers
- CA 19-9 is not sensitive enough for screening

52. Suspected PSC obtain a 3D MRI/MRCP with T1w and T2w axial images and contrast
- If normal then liver biopsy to rule out small-duct PSC under antibiotic coverage
- Repeat MRI/MRCP in 1 year if the diagnosis remains unclear
- ERCP should be avoided for the diagnosis of PSC
- No liver biopsy in typical findings on MRCP, except AIH overlap

53. In all possible PSC, serum IgG4 levels should be measured to exclude IgG4-SC

54. *Ileocolonoscopy in new PSC and no previous diagnosis of IBD*
    - Without IBD, next ileocolonoscopy at 5-years or with symptoms
    - PSC + IBD surveillance colonoscopy at age 15 years and repeat q1- 2 years

55. Small-duct PSC monitored by MRI/MRCP q 3–5 years for large-duct disease

56. In PSC with elevated ALP or GGT, UDCA 13–23 mg/kg/day can be considered for treatment and continued if there is a response
    - No oral vancomycin for the treatment of PSC

57. PSC with cirrhosis should undergo HCC surveillance

58. ERCP in PSC may be indicated for
    - Evaluation of relevant strictures
    - New-onset or worsening pruritus
    - Unexplained weight loss
    - Worsening serum liver test abnormalities
    - Rising serum CA 19-9
    - Recurrent bacterial cholangitis
    - Progressive bile duct dilation

59. MRI/MRCP should be considered prior to ERCP in PSC
    - Antimicrobial prophylaxis periprocedure
    - When a biliary stent is placed, stent removal within 4 weeks

60. Bile acid sequestrants should be used for pruritus in PSC that does not respond to heat avoidance, emollients, and antihistamines
    - Alternatives for refractory pruritus include
        - Sertraline 100 mg daily
        - Naltrexone 50–100 mg daily
        - Rifampin 150–300 mg twice daily

61. Active management of IBD and surveillance of colon cancer should continue in the post-transplant period in PSC

62. Fat-soluble vitamin levels checked at PSC diagnosis and yearly
    - Bone density examinations to exclude osteopenia or osteoporosis at diagnosis and at 2-3 year intervals

63. Liver transplantation (LT) should be considered in all patients with PSC with
    - End-stage liver disease
    - Recurrent cholangitis
    - Intractable pruritus

- Early-stage HCC

64. Hilar cholangiocarcinoma
   - Limit injection of contrast
   - No injection or stenting of atrophied segments
   - Drainage of all injected segments
   - Aim to drain > 50% of viable liver volume
   - Periprocedural antibiotics

65. Risks for cholangiocarcinoma
   - Asbestos
   - Smoking
   - Choledochal cysts
   - Caroli's disease
   - Exposure to thorotrast (thorium dioxide)

65. In hilar cholangiocarcinoma photodynamic therapy (PDT) or Radiofrequency ablation (RFA) of the tumors through metal stents can be considered
   - Metal stents > plastic stents for less intervention
   - In unresectable hilar tumor, bilateral stents > unilateral stents
   - Endoscopic approach better than percutaneous for preoperative drainage
   - In unresectable lesions, both approaches acceptable

66. Visual cholangioscopic impression of a bile duct stricture has the highest sensitivity in detection of cholangiocarcinoma

67. Cholangiocarcinoma with PTC
   - Primary bile salts synthesized from cholesterol. So with PTC cholesterol level is decreased
   - URSO increased bile output
   -Reduced chenodeoxycholic acid and deoxycholic acid since they are converted from primary bile acids in the gut and reabsorbed
   - Cholestyramine (Questran) worsens diarrhea by bile acid binding

68. GB polyps > 1 cm refer to surgery
   - Less than 1 cm follow up in 6-12 months except in PSC, GB polyp >8 mm sent to surgery
   - Large GB polyp (> 18 mm) treated by **open** cholecystectomy with liver and lymph node dissection

69. If patient > 60 years of age or Indian ethnicity or sessile polyp with thickening of GB wall > 4mm

- GB polyp </= 5 mm, US at 6 months and then annually
- GB polyp between 6-9 mm then cholecystectomy

70. Patient with no inherent risk of GB cancer
    - GB polyp < 6 mm without wall thickening or symptoms, no follow up (according to uptodate, repeat annually)

71. Gallbladder (GB) cancer
    - Highest risk in native Americans
    - Increased with large gallstones
    - Adenomyomatosis and cholesterolosis - NO increased risk of GB cancer
    - Porcelain gallbladder is a known risk of GB cancer refer to surgery
    - GB polyps > 1 cm

72. CCA and gallbladder carcinoma surveillance annually with MRI +/- Ca 19-9
    - No surveillance for PSC <18 years of age or with small-duct PSC
    - Cytology and FISH during ERCP for relevant strictures
    - Cholecystectomy for PSC with gallbladder polyps >8 mm
    - Polyps ≤8 mm monitored by US q 6 months
    - Ca 19-9 alone or PET scan should not be used to diagnose CCA

73. Adjuvant capecitabine should be considered for all CCA

74. *No EUS-guided FNA or percutaneous biopsy of a perihilar mass*
    - If LT is not an option, EUS-guided FNA can be diagnostic
    - pCCA for LT, EUS-FNA of regional LNs can be performed

75. Patients undergoing resection for p(perihilar)CCA or d(distal) CCA, preoperative endoscopic drainage of the remnant liver if biliary obstruction is present

76. LT following neoadjuvant therapy in pCCA (≤3 cm in radial diameter) that is unresectable or arising in the setting of PSC
    - Systemic chemotherapy is the first-line treatment of advanced CCA.
    - Gem/cis Platin is the standard of care for newly diagnosed patients
    - FOLFOX is appropriate second-line therapy

77. Intraductal papillary neoplasm of the bile duct (IPMN-B)
    - Mucin production in bile duct
    - Low incidence in the west, more common in far east
    - Leads to obstruction and dilation of bile duct
    - May progress to dysplasia and cholangiocarcinoma
    - Important precursor of cholangiocarcinoma
    - Type 1- mucous production, Type 2 without mucus production, type 3 is

multifocal, type 4 is superficially spreading

78. brushings have a yield of 50%- repeat brushing or choledochoscopy with biopsy directed

79. Fully covered metal stents have higher risk of migration than plastic biliary stents in the treatment of benign CBD strictures
    - Strictures recur at the same rate
    - Cholecystitis and pancreatitis not usually seen

80. Post transplant biliary strictures ERCP preferred over PTC

81. For anastomotic strictures, covered metal stents over plastic stents
    - Anastomotic strictures just below bifurcation may need plastic stents
    - Check MRCP in liver transplant receipt with suspected biliary stricture

82. Early post transplantation biliary stricture due to ischemia is managed by stent placement

83. IV antibiotics in those patients where complete drainage is technically challenging due to ischemic cholangitis, multiple strictures and failure of stenting

84. Milwaukee system of SOD type 1, 2, 3 is outdated
    - SOD 1 now labelled papillary stenosis
    - SOD 2- Functional biliary sphincter disorder associated with abnormal biochemistry or duct changes
    - SOD 3- Functional biliary type pain- no role for ERCP

Pancreatic cysts

1. Pancreatic cyst
    - Size < 1 cm = MRI in 2 years
    - Size 1-2 cm = MRI in 1 year
    - Size 2-3 cm = MRI in 6-12 months
    - Size > 3 cm = Multidisciplinary group and EUS

2. Pancreatic cyst > 3 cm with dilated pancreatic duct go for EUS or MRI surveillance
    - > 3 cm MRI in 6-12 months
    - Pancreatic cysts with at least 2 high-risk features, such as size ≥3 cm, a dilated main pancreatic duct, or the presence of an associated solid component, should be examined with EUS-FNA (AGA 2015)

3. Incidental pancreatic cyst seen on chest CT, repeat imaging with dedicated CT or MRI of the pancreas

4. Pancreatic cyst in a patient who is poor surgical risk, no further work up or surveillance

5. Symptomatic pancreatic cyst needs to be referred to surgery regardless of underlying pathology

5. Pancreatic cysts features
    - Unilocular cyst with communication with PD is a side branch IPMN
    - Numerous cysts (honeycombed appearance) and/ or Central scar is serous cystadenoma, no further work up
        - Serous cystadenoma cells positive for glycogen
    - Hx of pancreatitis, consider a Pseudocyst
    - Mucinous cyst has no communication with PD

6. Pancreatic cyst with a calcified wall is consistent with mucinous cystadenoma or carcinoma.
    - Usually in the tail
    - Female
    - Treatment is surgery

7. Patient with > 3 cm pancreatic cyst with small mural nodule with elevated CEA levels. Treatment is surgery

8. Patients with both a solid component and a dilated pancreatic duct and/or concerning features on EUS and FNA should undergo surgery to reduce the

risk of mortality from carcinoma. (AGA 2015)

9. Cyst with invasive cancer or dysplasia s/p surgery should undergo MRI surveillance of any remaining pancreas every 2 years
    - No routine surveillance of pancreatic cysts without high-grade dysplasia or malignancy at surgical resection (AGA 2015)

10. Patients with pancreatitis and a large cyst already formed at presentation, the next step is EUS

11. CT imaging with 2 densities with pancreatic pseudocyst
    - Check hematocrit (Hct) for a pseudoaneurysm/ bleed into the pseudocyst
    - Chronic pancreatitis with pseudocyst with pseudoaneurysm needs angiography

12. Antibiotics needed for EUS guided FNA of pancreatic cyst

13. Asymptomatic pseudocyst - conservative management

14. Fisheye appearance of major papilla is IPMN
    - Equal in males and females

15. Von-Hippel Lindau disease
    - Renal cancers, blindness and incidental pancreatic cyst

16. Kras mutation in cyst favor mucinous differentiation
    - CEA levels in cysts > 800 are specific for IPMN and mucinous cysts

Pancreatitis

1. Harmless acute pancreatitis score (HAPS) for pancreatitis
   - Normal creatinine
   - Normal Hct
   - No rebound

2. Amylase is non-specific and normalizes faster than lipase in acute pancreatitis.
   - Triglyceride elevation can cause spuriously low amylase.
   - Amylase levels over 1k are reliable for diagnosis of acute pancreatitis

3. Idiopathic pancreatitis > 40 years of age needs an EUS
   - First episode of idiopathic pancreatitis with a history of smoking and new onset DM needs CT or MRI cross sectional imaging

4. Autoimmune pancreatitis type 1
   - Seen in 6-7th decade with male predominance
   - Associated with PSC, retroperitoneal fibrosis, Sjogren's
   - Lymphoplasmacytic sclerosing pattern, storiform fibrosis and chronic lymphocytic infiltration surrounding pancreatic duct
       - > 10 IgG4-positive cells with at least 2 of the following:
          - Periductal lymphoplasmacytic infiltrate
          - Obliterative phlebitis
          - Swirling collagen fibers (storiform fibrosis)
   - Increased IgG4; increased IgG4 plasma cells in the pancreas
   - Pancreatogram with skinny beaded pancreatic duct
   - CT shows sausage shaped pancreas and irregular thin pancreatic duct
   - Treat with steroids; next in line is Rituximab

5. Autoimmune pancreatitis associated with
   - Salivary gland issues (sialadenitis- Mikulicz disease)
   - PSC
   - Adenopathy
   - Mediastinal fibrosis
   - Aortic aneurysm and periaortitis
   - Tubulointerstitial nephritis

6. Autoimmune pancreatitis type 2
   - Young with equal prevalence in males and females
   - Associated with inflammatory bowel disease.
   - IgG4 level is normal or mildly elevated.
   - Pathology shows a granulocytic epithelial lesion in the pancreatic duct

(duct centric) with minimal IgG4-positive cells

7. Binge drinking doesn't cause Alcoholic pancreatitis
   - Brief alcohol intervention during admission

8. Small duct pancreatitis
   - No steatorrhea, No calcifications
   - No Alcohol use, Equivocal EUS/ MRCP/ ERCP
   - Diagnosis by endoscopic secretion tests

9. Most convincing evidence for drug induced pancreatitis is for
   - Mesalamine, Estrogens, Valproic acid and AZT/6 MP
     - Mesalamine with pancreatitis usually after 4-8 weeks of treatment

10. Pancreatitis is a non-dose dependent idiosyncratic reaction of AZT/ 6MP

11. Acute pancreatitis from hypertriglyceridemia
    - Vit A and isotretinoin
    - Thiazides
    - Beta-blockers
    - Estrogens
    - Alcohol

12. HIV associated medications causing pancreatitis
    - Didanosine
    - Pentamidine
    - Dapsone
    - Bactrim
    - Furosemide
    - Metronidazole
    - Nelfinavir

13. Severe pancreatitis
    - Age > 55 years
    - BMI> 30
    - Evidence of organ failure
    - Hemoconcentration
    - Pleural effusion
    - Early CT scan can underestimate the severity of acute pancreatitis

14. Treatment of pancreatitis is
    - Aggressive IV hydration (> 250 cc per hour)
    - PCA pump analgesia
    - Close monitoring.

- If any evidence of worsening, then ICU transfer for aggressive hydration, rule out infection then antibiotics with a potential for CT guided aspiration of pancreas

15. Necrotizing pancreatitis and infected necrosis
    - Early is usually sterile
    - ⅓ will have infections/ sepsis after 10-14 days
    - Treatment is carbapenem

16. In necrotizing pancreatitis, reduced mortality if surgery postponed to 4 weeks with antibiotics. Surgery for septic necrosis after 2-4 weeks while aseptic necrosis after 4-6 weeks
    - Continue Antibiotics and current management in a clinically stable infected necrosis for 2-4 weeks prior to surgery
    - EUS guided FNA an option to evaluate the pancratic necrosis for infection
        - No need for CT guided FNA in infected necrosis
    - Liquefaction of necrosis occur by 4-5 weeks

17. Nasogastric feeds has same results as nasojejunal feeds usually after 4-7 days after admission

18. Enteral feeding in pancreatitis reduces bacterial translocation from the gut

18. No prophylactic antibiotics for sterile necrosis

19. Step up approach with endoscopic necrosectomy first followed by surgical necrosectomy

20. Pancreatic walled off necrosis (WON) if no symptoms then no interventions
    - Initial treatment of infected necrosis is broad spectrum antibiotics

21. Liraglutide GLP-1 Agonist to treat DM2 has increased risk of amylase/ lipase elevation
    - Also causes constipation

22. Commonest ERCP finding in Pancreatitis is normal pancreatogram

23. Persistent organ failure > 48 hours in acute pancreatitis has highest risk of death

24. Pancreatic pleural effusion in chronic pancreatitis or Pancreatic-pleural fistula with pleural effusion, treat with ERCP and pancreatic stent

25. There is no RCT for fluids in acute pancreatitis

26. Eluxadoline (Viberzi) for IBS constipation causes pancreatitis

27. P divisum can be diagnosed by EUS and present in 5-10% of general population

28. Severe pancreatitis with duct disruption, place a PD stent with an internal and external flange even when the guide wire does not get beyond the disruption
   - PD with leak after pancreatic surgery, treat with pancreatic duct stenting

29. Disconnected duct syndrome
   - Hx of pancreatitis with associated with necrosis around downstream pancreatic duct
   - Functioning upstream pancreatic parenchyma
   - Post prandial fullness and fluid collection in upstream pancreas
   - Can lead to fistulae and recurrent pancreatitis
   - Needs surgery for resection or internal drainage procedure
   - Plastic stents have been placed for up to year endoscopically

30. 3rd day after pancreatitis, trial of PO intake

31. Chronic pancreatitis with dilated pancreatic duct, *long term relief better with surgery*

32. Pancreatic stone seen on EUS is diagnostic of chronic pancreatitis

33. Patient with chronic pancreatitis with weight loss, calcifications, dilated PD, CT scan showing atrophy but no mass
   - Test for elastase and treat for malabsorption before looking for cancer

34. Pain of chronic pancreatitis
   - Placebo response is 40%
   - Pregabalin or Lyrica is helpful
   - *Pancreatic enzymes not recommended per guidelines*

35. B12 deficiency seen in chronic pancreatitis
   - R factor produced by salive binds to B12 and needs to be cleaved

- Low stool elastase associated with chronic pancreatitis

36. Chronic calcific pancreatitis with dilated CBD and Portal vein clot and cavernous transformation
   - After failed multiple plastic stents, treat with fully covered metal stent
   - Cavernous transformation - non-surgical candidate. Varicose veins are a relative contraindication for surgery
   - Chronic pancreatitis with dilated PD with varices/ vascular collaterals with symptoms such as pain- treat with ERCP with dilation and sphincterotomy.

37. Middle aged patient with steatorrhea and normal D-xylose has pancreatic insufficiency

38. Inhibitory and pain fibers from the pancreas go through sympathetic nerves
   - Vagus has parasympathetic nerves
   - Celiac ganglia have sympathetic nerves

39. Rectal indomethacin suppositories before the procedure reduces post ERCP pancreatitis

40. PD stent damages pancreatic duct and parenchyma

41. Increased post ERCP pancreatitis in patients with
   - Normal T Bili
   - Female
   - Young patients
   - SOD
   - Hx of recurrent pancreatitis
   - Past history of ERCP induced pancreatitis
   - Pancreatic duct injection, pancreatic interventions, failed prophylactic pancreatic duct stenting
   - Post ERCP pancreatitis worse with normal pancreatogram

42. Factors not causing risk of post-ERCP pancreatitis include
   - Duodenal diverticulum
   - *Small CBD*
   - Intramural contrast injection
   - P divisum
   - Previous failed ERCP
   - Allergy to contrast

43. In ampullectomy, pancreatic stent placement after ampullectomy

44. Acid in the duodenum helps release secretin from pancreas which produces bicarb rich fluid to neutralize the acid
- Aminoacids and fat in the duodenum helps release cholecystokinin that helps release pancreatic enzymes
- Carbohydrates helps release amylase from pancreas

45. Patient with chronic pancreatitis under treatment for exocrine insufficiency check DEXA scan

46. Young patient with recurrent pancreatitis needs genetic testing
- Cationic trypsinogen gene (PRSS1)
    - Autosomal dominant and most common if multiple family members involved
    - Gain of function mutation with activation of trypsin
- Anionic trypsinogen gene (PRSS2)
- Serine protease inhibitor Kazal 1 gene (SPINK1)
- Cystic fibrosis transmembrane conductance regulator gene (CFTR)
    - Young patient with azoospermia (infertility) and pancreatitis, sweat chloride test for cystic fibrosis
- Chymotrypsinogen C gene (CTRC)
- Calcium sensing receptor gene (CASR)

47. Exocrine pancreatic insufficiency is the commonest pancreatic issue with cystic fibrosis

48. Correction of steatorrhea with pancreatic enzyme supplements also leads to correction of carbohydrate and protein malabsorption

49. Shwachman-Diamond syndrome
- Skeletal abnormalities
- Neutropenia with cyclic infection
- Growth retardation
- Pancreatic insufficiency without chronic pancreatitis
- AR with gene on chromosome 7
- Down's syndrome associated with annular pancreas but not Shwachman syndrome

50. Down's syndrome associated with annular pancreas which is incomplete rotation of ventral and dorsal pancreatic buds leading to gastric outlet obstruction

51. CT/MRI is the first line in the diagnosis of chronic pancreatitis (CP) (ACG 2020)

- Secretin MRCP (s-MRCP) only if cross sectional imaging or EUS is non-diagnostic
- Histology is the gold standard

52. Stop alcohol and smoking in CP
    - Use antioxidants but not pancreatic enzymes in CP
    - Celiac plexus block for pain relief in CP

53. Pancreatic enzymes replacement therapy in CP with exocrine pancreatic insufficiency
    - Pancreatic enzyme supplementation 40-50k lipase units going up to 90K
    - Periodic evaluation for osteoporosis and fat soluble vitamin deficiency
    - Development of DM in CP is related to duration of disease and other risks such as BMI, smoking etc.

54. Total pancreatectomy with autologous islet cell transplantation (TPIAT)
    - Radical treatment of patients at high risk of pancreatic cancer such as hereditary pancreatitis or intractable pain in young patients from chronic pancreatitis
    - >50% 1 year narcotic free
    - 35% 1-year insulin free which reduced with time
    - Stable blood sugars

55. EUS is the preferred diagnostic test for unexplained acute and chronic pancreatitis. MRI/MRCP is an alternative (AGA 2022)

56. ERCP with P Divisum
    - Dilated dorsal pancreatic duct
    - Santorinicele
    - There is no role for ERCP to treat pain alone in pancreas divisum.

57. ERCP controversial in idiopathic recurrent acute pancreatitis and standard pancreatic ductal anatomy is controversial
    - Biliary sphincterotomy preferable to dual sphincterotomy.

58. *Surgical intervention over endoscopic therapy for long-term treatment of obstructive chronic pancreatitis with dilated PD*

59. ERCP with conventional stone extraction in small (≤5mm) main pancreatic duct stones
    - Larger stones need extracorporeal shockwave lithotripsy and/or pancreatoscopy with intraductal lithotripsy
    - ERCP with prolonged stent therapy (6-12 months) is effective for treating and remodeling main pancreatic duct strictures.

- Fully covered metal stents may have a role
- Fully covered metal stent placement is favored over multiple plastic stents whenever feasible

60. Celiac plexus block should not be routinely performed for the management of pain due to chronic pancreatitis

61. Rectal NSAIDS > 30 minutes before or during ERCP

62. Wire guided cannulation over contrast guided cannulation
IV hydration 20 mg/ kg bolus followed by 3 ml/kg/hr

63. Splenic artery aneurysm greater than 2 cm is coil embolization
   - Hemosuccus pancreaticus (blood loss through pancreatic duct) indicative of splenic artery aneurysm

64. D-xylose test depends on Gastric emptying, small bowel absorbtion and Renal clearance

65. Pancreatic function test: measuring duodenal bicarbonate after IV secretin.

Pancreatic neoplasm

1. Pancreatic cancer screening annually with genetic susceptibility
   - Individuals with 1 first-degree relative (FDR) with pancreatic cancer who in turn also has a FDR with pancreatic cancer (familial pancreatic cancer kindred)
   - Peutz-Jeghers Syndrome (PJS)
       - Highest risk of pancreatic cancer is Puetz-Jeghers syndrome or STK11 mutation
       - Start screening age 35 years
   - CDKN2A (P16), BRCA, PALB2, ATM, Lynch (MLH1, MSH2 or MSH6) with 1 FDR with pancreatic cancer

2. Familial atypical multiple mole melanoma (FAMMM) involves CDKN2A mutation

3. Hereditary breast and ovarian cancer syndrome associated with BRCA2 gene mutation. Increased risk of pancreatic cancer with family history of pancreatic cancer

4. Pancreatic cancer screening with EUS alternating with MRI, or MRI based on patient preference and available expertise (ASGE 2022)
   - EUS is the initial screening test for PJS and FAMMM

5. EUS can be combined with screening upper endoscopy or colonoscopy (eg, Lynch and Peutz-Jeghers syndrome)
   - MRI may be combined with enterography for PJS

6. Age 50 or 10 years earlier than the youngest relative with pancreatic cancer.
   - BRCA2
   - BRCA1
   - PALB2
   - FPC syndrome
   - Screening for all first degree relatives
   - Heterozygotes for Ataxia Telangiectasia Mutated (ATM) pathogenic variant with first- or second-degree relative with pancreatic cancer
   - Lynch syndrome with first- or second-degree relative with pancreatic cancer

7. Age 40 or 10 years earlier than the youngest relative with pancreatic cancer
   - FAMMM syndrome
   - Autosomal-dominant hereditary pancreatitis

8. Age 35 or 10 years earlier than the youngest relative with pancreatic cancer
  - Peutz-Jeghers syndrome

9. Pancreatic mass with steatorrhea- Somatostatinoma
  - Pancreatic mass with necrolytic migratory erythema skin rash and weight loss- Glucagonoma
  - Pancreatic mass with weight gain and hypoglycemia - insulinoma

10. Whipple's triad for insulinoma
  - Symptoms of hypoglycemia, low blood sugar and relief with sugar load

11. Painless obstructive jaundice next step is to obtain an EUS to r/o pancreatic cancer
  - Dilated PD is not autoimmune pancreatitis but likely to be pancreatic cancer
  - PD is tiny in autoimmune pancreatitis

12. Insulinomas are an uncommon part of MEN syndrome and are usually benign
  - Insulinoma is often sporadic, cured by surgery

13. Patient with metastatic pancreatic cancer with metal stent and hemobilia with no Interventional Radiology embolization target
  - Place a second metal stent (coated) for Tamponade
  - IR embolization if target available

14. Hemobilia managed by angiography with embolization

15. Quincke's triad of GI bleed, RUQ pain and jaundice consistent with hemobilia

16. CFTR gene mutation has no increased risk of pancreatic cancer

17. Risk of malignancy with branch duct IPMN
  - Symptomatic such as back pain
  - Nodules
  - > 3 cm
  - PD > 6 mm

18. Patients with new onset DM are at a higher risk of pancreatic cancer if
  - Age > 65
  - Smoker
  - Nonobese status at diagnosis
  - Hx of chronic pancreatitis

19. Pancreatic cancer with liver lesions
    - US guided liver biopsy
    - ERCP with bare metal stent

20. Glucagonoma
    - Pancreatic tumor and necrolytic migratory erythema
        - Biopsies show superficial necrolysis with separation of outer layers and perivascular infiltration with lymphocytes and histiocytes
    - DM, weight loss, **diarrhea, DVT**, cheilosis and Necrolytic migratory erythema
    - Almost always within pancreas and Unresectable
    - Levels > 1000pg
    - Fasting blood sugar > 200

21. MEN 1
    - p-NET in 80%
    - Gastrinomas in 50% - causes ZE syndrome
    - Insulinomas in 20%

22. Somatostatinoma causes osmotic diarrhea while Medullary carcinoma of thyroid causes secretory diarrhea
    - MEN1 involves parathyroid, pituitary and pancreas
    - MEN2 involves Medullary carcinoma of thyroid, parathyroid and pheochromocytoma

23. NET have markers such as synaptophysin, chromogranin A, and CD56

24. IPMN main duct dilation > 10 mm then surgery
    - PD > 5 mm is of concern

25. P-NET with solitary met managed via surgery

8. MISCELLANEOUS

Infections

1. Coccidioidomycosis
   - Southwestern US such as New Mexico

2. Histoplasmosis
   - Ohio and Mississippi river valley

3. Weil's syndrome
   - Leptospirosis
   - Swimming in fresh water or exposure to sewage
   - Transmitted through urine of small rodents
   - Conjunctivitis, jaundice, fevers, diarrhea, headaches, renal insufficiency, temperature -pulse dissociation, rhabdomyolysis
   - Serology ELISA test
   - Doxycycline for treatment

4. Shiga toxin producing E coli infection not treated with antibiotics due to Hemolytic uremic syndrome (HUS)
   - Cholera treated with tetracycline
   - Shigella with Cipro

5. Hemolytic uremic syndrome presents with AKI, hemolytic anemia and thrombocytopenia

6. Plain film showing air in the portal tree indicates Ischemic bowel disease

7. Syphilis treatment
   - Benzathine penicillin 2.4 million units IM or doxycycline x 14 days

8. Visiting tropical country + Duodenal villi flattened is Tropical Sprue
   - Treated with tetracycline + Folic acid x 3-6 months
   - Macrocytic anemia, B12 and folate deficiency, normal Fe levels, increased fecal fat
   - Biopsies show villous blunting with negative celiac disease

9. HIV positive with pathology slide showing a large cell with a large nucleus is CMV
   - Dark intranuclear inclusion body on slides. Also, perinuclear halo, intranuclear inclusions and cytoplasmic inclusions
   - Treatment is ganciclovir
   - HSV treated with acyclovir

- Schistosomiasis treated with Praziquantel

10. Asian or Vietnam POW with change in mental status after anticancer therapy or middle aged visitor to far east with eosinophilia and diarrhea with weight loss
   - Strongyloides hyperinfection
   - Not always associated with eosinophilia
   - Test is serology. Check serology for Strongyloides
   - Strongyloides treated with Ivermectin
   - Human T cell lymphotropic virus type 1 is a risk factor for Strongyloides infection

11. Large volume diarrhea associated with small bowel disease
   - Raspberries/ Strawberries associated with Cyclospora after 1 week's incubation
   - Treated with Bactrim for 1 week
   - Incubation for Staph, B ceres and norovirus is much shorter

12. Norovirus
   - Associated with fruits vegetables, mollusks
   - Hard to contain due to small inoculums, high infectivity, stability and protracted viral shedding mean duration of 4 weeks
   - Spread through fecal oral route, fomites and aerosolized vomiting
   - Incubation is 1-2 days
   - Lasts 3-7 days
   - Norovirus has no lifelong immunity

13. Recurrent C diff
   - Treat with Vanco x 10 days at 125 mg
   - If Vanco used initially use fidaxomicin x 10 days
   - If fulminant C diff
      - PO vancomycin at 500 mg QID
      - IV Metronidazole
      - Vancomycin enemas if ileus
      - Surgery with complication
      - FMT if not a surgical candidate

14. Hydatid cyst (Echinococcus)
   - Eosinophilia, diagnosed through ELISA
   - Comes from dog feces (not sheep)
   - Albendazole/ Mebendazole and per cutaneous drainage
   - Polycystic liver disease associated with brain aneurysm

15. Ascaris at papilla

- Managed by sphincterotomy and balloon sweep
- Treated with albendazole
- Mebendazole for hookworms (Necator and Ancylostomiases)

16. Amoebic liver abscess
    - On CT appears like owl's eye
    - 10 x more in men
    - Hepatic abscess in less than 1% of intestinal infection
    - Only + in 40% of stool microscopy
    - Abscess + for organism in < 20%

17. Treatment of Entamoeba is Metronidazole
    - Paromomycin only after Metronidazole to treat intraluminal cysts
    - Causes flask like ulcers in the colon

18. Mebendazole to treat pinworms and hookworms

19. Patient with Kidney transplantation
    - Biopsies show intranuclear inclusion bodies in the mucosa is HSV
    - Acyclovir x 14 days if it fails then Foscarnet

20. Reduced CD4 count with diarrhea and abdominal pain
    - Check for cryptosporidium and microsporidia
    - Patient on HAART therapy for HIV - non opportunistic bacterial infection

21. Working in an animal farm with pain, fever, vomiting, systemic response inflammatory syndrome (SIRS), necrotic abdominal lymph nodes, ascites is Anthrax

22. Patient from far east with liver biopsy showing calcified parasite eggs, CT scan shows turtle back liver indicating capsular retraction and macronodular cirrhosis is schistosomiasis and treatment is Praziquantel

23. Albendazole is used for treatment of pinworms, hookworms, Whipworms, Trichuriasis
    - Triclabendazole is used for treatment of Fasciola Hepatica
    - Metronidazole for Amoebic abscess

24. Trichuris trichiura causes rectal prolapse if stool burden is large

25. Enterobius vermicularis causes pruritus ani and can be treated with Mebendazole or Albendazole

26. Treatment of Campylobacter in pregnant women is Azithromycin

27. Young person with history of travel with erythema nodosum, arthralgia and CT showing terminal ileitis as well as bulky mesenteric lymphadenopathy indicates Yersinia enterocolitica
- Presents with prolonged diarrhea. When diarrhea stops, arthritis and sore throat starts
- May cause Reiter's syndrome which is arthritis, urethritis and conjunctivitis
- Yersinia enterocolitica mimics CD with bulky lymphadenopathy, longer course and treated with Bactrim, aminoglycosides, doxycycline and Fluroquinolones
- Yersinia is siderophilic and can be worse in hereditary hemochromatosis and thalassemia
- Treat with antibiotics for extraintestinal manifestations

28. Reactive arthritis occurring after acute gastroenteritis associated with HLA B-27
- Caused by Yersinia, Salmonella, Shigella, Campylobacter
- Chlamydia

29. C diff - prevent recurrent C diff with washing hands and shower to reduce spores on skin
- Commonest cause of death from GI infection

30. Vibrio Vulnificus presents with bullous skin lesions and septicemia is associated with shellfish
- Cellulitis in HIV, elevated iron storage disorder or cirrhosis
- Septicemia and septic shock
- Treatment is with doxycycline and third generation cephalosporins

31. Lymphogranuloma venereum (LGV) is caused by chlamydia trachomatis and diagnosis is through serology or NAAT
- Rectal proctitis upto 10 cm
- Stage 1 which is from 3-30 days presents as local inflammation
- Stage 2 from 2-6 weeks shows constitutional symptoms
- Stage 3 is abscess and fistula
- Treat with doxycycline x 3 weeks or Erythromycin/Azithromycin

32. Raw beef causes Taenia saginata treated with Praziquantel or Niclosamide

33. Patient with transplantation develops systemic symptoms such as fever,

abdominal pain, nausea and vomiting with odynophagia
- CMV causes systemic symptoms and not candida or HSV

34. Raspberry dessert with 7-day incubation period followed by explosive diarrhea (small bowel origin) is Cyclospora

35. Slide with triangular organism consistent with giardia. May cause steatorrhea

36. Mycobacterium avium intracellulare affects HIV patients with low CD4 count with severe systemic symptoms, fever, diarrhea, weight loss, bulky mesenteric lymph nodes and frosted yellowish plaques involving the small bowel

37. E Coli affecting small bowel
   - Enterotoxigenic EC- Traveler's diarrhea
   - Enteropathogenic EC - Diarrhea in children
   - Enteroadherent E Coli cause diarrhea in AIDS (and children)

38. E Coli affecting colon
   - Enteroinvasive EC and Enterohemorrhagic E coli
   - Shiga Toxin
   - Severe diarrhea O157:H7, hemolytic uremic syndrome
   - Avoid antibiotics and antidiarrheals

39. Kaposi's sarcoma in HIV caused by Herpesvirus 8 and associated with low CD4 counts
   - Management is by initiating antiretroviral therapy

40. Biphasic diarrhea (watery followed by dysentery) without systemic symptoms but WBC in stools is campylobacter and shigella
   - Shigella associated with daycare exposure

41. Yersinia and C diff often cause non-bloody diarrhea

42. Food poisoning associated with
   - S aureus
   - B cereus (associated with rice)
   - C perfringens

43. C perfringens food poisoning
   - Within 5 hours of eating

- Associated with meats and beef
- Diarrhea and abdominal cramping lasting 24 hours
- No vomiting

44. Staph aureus food poisoning
   - Meat and poultry
   - Vomiting

45. Listeria is associated with dairy and causes gastroenteritis.
   - Associated with improperly cooked hot dogs
   - Worse outcomes in pregnant women and immunocompromised individuals
   - Diagnosed via blood cultures

46. Large volume diarrhea after camping is Giardia or Cryptosporidium (in immunocompromised)
   - Doesn't involve colon

47. Cryptosporidium treated by nitazoxanide x 3 days
   Causes profuse nonbloody diarrhea

48. Following camping patient presents with aches, pains and low volume watery diarrhea likely has viral gastroenteritis

49. Alpha-gal syndrome
   - Alpha-gal syndrome related to increased alpha-gal IgE antibodies
   - Abdominal pain, diarrhea with nausea and vomiting with mammalian products
   - Associated with Lone star tick bites (Amblyoma americanum)
   - Avoid non-primate mammalian products including meat, milk etc, avoid tick bites and allergy referral

50. Rotavirus is a live vaccine and avoided in infants of mothers who got anti-TNF for IBD

51. Blastocystis hominis in immunosuppressed individuals treated with Flagyl
   - Often asymptomatic
   - No treatment in asymptomatic patients

52. Cystoisospora bellie
   - Tropics and subtropics
   - 1-2 weeks of incubation
   - Immucompetent hosts and institutionalized hosts

- Watery diarrhea with transient fever 2-3 weeks
- Associated with eosinophilia
- Treated with Bactrim

Anticoagulation

1. Low risk of embolization (i.e., non-valvular paroxysmal A fib)
   - No need for bridge anticoagulation with heparin
   - Stop warfarin 5 days without any bridge therapy

2. With a high risk of thromboembolism and uncontrolled GI bleed, OK to hold warfarin for 4-7 days without increasing the risk of thromboembolism
   - Anticoagulation in high risk patients should not be held beyond 5-7 days due to high risk of of thromboembolic events

3. 4 factor prothrombin complexes used to reverse the INR in warfarin induced supratherapeutic INR

4. Age is the highest risk for anticoagulant associated GI bleed

5. Andexanet alfa (Andexxa)
   - Antidote for Rivaroxaban (Xarelto) and Apixaban (Eliquis)
   - Modified human Xa decoy protein
   - Reversal of direct acting anticoagulant avoided since it increases the risk of thromboembolism

6. Cardiology patient with UGIB INR of 2.5
   - Do not give Vitamin K that has been associated with thromboembolic events
   - Threshold to transfuse these patients is lower

7. Apixaban held for 2 days, Warfarin held for 5 days prior to colonoscopy/endoscopic procedure

8. A normal PT rules out toxic levels of rivaroxaban or Edoxaban
   - Normal PT doesn't rule out toxic levels of Apixaban- Needs drug specific assay

9. Dabigatran (Pradaxa) toxicity can be ruled out via diluted thrombin time, aPTT or ecarin clotting time

10. Dabigatran has the highest risk of GI bleed among direct acting oral anticoagulants

11. Warfarin with acute GI bleeding, prothrombin complex concentrate administration over FFP

- No vitamin K
- NO FFP

12. No idarucizumab for patients on dabigatran with acute GI bleeding,
    - No Andexanet alfa for patients on rivaroxaban or apixaban with acute GI bleeding
    - No prothrombin complex concentrate for direct oral anticoagulants with acute GI bleeding

13. No platelet transfusions for patients on antiplatelet agents with acute GI bleeding

14. Do not hold ASA for patients with GI bleeding on cardiac ASA
    - Resume ASA on the day hemostasis is endoscopically confirmed
    - Upper GI Bleed with aspirin for primary prophylaxis but no cardiovascular risks, aspirin can be stopped following GI bleed

15. Continue warfarin for elective/planned GI procedures
    - No bridging anticoagulation if warfarin is held

16. Interrupt direct oral anticoagulants (DOACs) for elective endoscopic GI procedures

17. Dual antiplatelet therapy undergoing elective GI procedures, interrupt the P2Y12 inhibitor while continuing ASA
    - Do not interrupt ASA 81–325 mg/d (monotherapy) for secondary cardiovascular prevention

Statistics

1. Number needed to treat is 1/ absolute risk (AR)
    - For example: Drug risk is 0.7% i.e., 7 out of 1000 risk
    Placebo risk is 0.3% i.e., 3 out of 1000 risk
    AR is the Difference between the two risks i.e., 7-3/1000 = 4/1000
    Number needed to treat (NNT) = 1/AR = 1000/4 = 1 out of 250

2. Relative risk = Risk of treatment- (minus) risk of placebo/ (divided by) risk of placebo
    - Relative risk reduction is Risk of placebo- risk of medication / (divided by) risk of placebo
    - Absolute risk reduction is Risk of placebo- Risk of intervention

Potpourri

1. Avoidant restrictive food eating disorder should be considered in young patients with GI complaints with weight loss and restrictive diet.
    - Refer to psychiatry and dietary consultation

2. Obesity
    - Increases the risk of CRC, pancreatic cancer, stomach cancer and liver cancer

3. ASA 4
    - Renal failure not on dialysis
    - Decompensated CHF

4. Hereditary hemorrhagic telangiectasia (Osler-Weber-Rendu disease)
    - Autosomal dominant
    - If hematochezia, then likely not HHT. Look for another source such as diverticular bleed
        - Elderly patient with Hematochezia likely to be diverticular bleed
    - UGI bleed likely presents with melena and hematemesis. Source usually in stomach or small bowel (duodenal bulb)/ not in the colon. Melena > Hematochezia
    - 70% have bleeding episodes by age 16. However serious bleeding/ Hemorrhage only after 4th decade
    - When liver is involved with liver vascular malformations may cause shunts, high output heart failure, portal hypertension with ascites/ variceal bleed, biloma and mesenteric ischemia
    - Chronic GI bleed may need double balloon enteroscopy if a small bowel angioectasia is detected

5. Acute intermittent porphyria (AIP)
    - Autosomal dominant
    - No family history
    - Females > Males
    - 20-30 years of age. Young patient with abdominal pain and convulsions with increased urine urobilinogen is AIP
    - Abdominal pain, fever, neuropathy, fever, psychiatric issues, SIADH and hyponatremia, leukocytosis, convulsions
    - No skin lesions
    - Attacks precipitated by fasting, low carb diet, sulfa, estrogens and alcohol
    - Test urine for porphobilinogen. Increased urinary porphyrin and porphobilinogen

- Definitive treatment is IV hemin, IV glucose and high Carbohydrate diet
- Definitive test decrease in RBC porphobilinogen deaminase
- Reduced porphobilinogen deaminase leading to increased ALA and porphobilinogen

6. Acute hepatic porphyria
- Women aged 15-50 years with recurrent severe abdominal pain should be screened
- Urine for aminolevulinic acid, porphobilinogen and creatinine
- Genetic testing with positive urine test
- Severe abdominal pain requiring hospitalization IV hemin through high flow central vein
- Avoid alcohol and porphyrinogenic medications
- Prophylactic heme therapy or givosiran if > 4 attacks per year
- Liver transplant only in those who are refractory to pharmaceutical therapy
- Monitor annually for liver disease
- At age 50 HCC screening starts
- Screen for kidney disease with creatinine and GFR

7. Methotrexate side effects
- Atypical pneumonia
- Pulmonary fibrosis
- BM suppression
- Liver enzyme abnormality

8. 6-MP side effects
-Neutropenia and Lymphopenia

9. Benzodiazepines/ midazolam with Grade D drug in Pregnancy

10. Eosinophilic gastroenteritis
- Malabsorption
- Diarrhea, obstruction, ulceration
- Ascites
- Differential diagnosis includes IBD, parasitic infections, drugs, vasculitis and malignancies such as leukemia, mastocytosis and lymphoma

11. Carcinoid has uniform monotonous appearing purple cells with cords and nests

12. Hereditary angioedema causes edema of the jejunal loop, abdominal pain OCP and ace inhibitors are the triggers
- Low C1 esterase inhibitor protein

- Affects larynx, gut and skin
- Treated with bradykinin antagonist such as icatibant or ecallantide

13. Acute hepatic porphyria treated with Givosiran

14. Serotonin is an excitatory neurostimulator stored in enteroendocrine cells. Acetylcholine excitatory but not stored
    - Nitric Oxide (NO) and pancreatic polypeptide are inhibitory

15. Korsakoff's syndrome
    - Ophthalmoplegia
    - Nystagmus, Ataxia

16. Elevated MMA and homocysteine indicate B12 deficiency and can be caused by chronic PPI use

17. Gastrografin and Barium
    - Gastrografin contraindicated in I2 allergy
    - Gastrografin bad for lungs
    - Barium bad for peritoneum (not used for suspected perforation)

18. Sodium is absorbed by 2 mechanisms in the gut
    - Na-Substrate mechanism
    - NaCl mechanism
        - NaCl mechanism may be impaired in cholera
    - Gatorade for sweat replacement and not diarrhea due to excess sugar and less electrolytes

19. Narrow angle glaucoma - dicyclomine is contraindicated

20. Vagal nerve stimulation
    - Receptive relaxation of proximal stomach
    - Acetylcholine release
        - Increased acid secretion by muscarinic receptors of parietal cells
        - Increase histamine release by ECL cells
        - Decreased somatostatin by stomach D cells
    - Increased gastrin by increased Gastrin releasing peptide from antral G cells

21. Pellagra in a patient with gastric bypass and skin rash
    - Rash over sun exposed skin

22. B6 (pyridoxine) deficiency presents stomatitis, glossitis, cheilosis, depression and peripheral neuropathy

23. Refeeding syndrome
- Cardiac, pulmonary and neuromuscular failure
- Fluid overload in phosphate deficiency or in thiamine deficiency
- Low levels of K and Mg
- Stop aggressive fluid intake and check phosphate
- TPN suddenly in a cachectic individual may cause CHF due to refeeding syndrome

24. Copper deficiency
- Hypochromic anemia, microcytic anemia, leukopenia, neutropenia
- With normal Fe and B12
- Associated with neurological symptoms such as ataxia and myeloneuropathy
- Cu deficiency can occur in Zn supplementation due to competitive absorption

25. Selenium deficiency causes cardiac and somatic muscle issues
- Heart and joint issues known as Kashin-Beck disease
- Myalgia and immune deficiencies

26. Peutz-Jeghers syndrome - *STK11/LKB 1* gene
- Pigmentation that decreases with age

27. Pruritus and facial swelling after eating, refer to an allergist

28. Familial Mediterranean Fever
- Serositis: Recurrent peritonitis, pleuritis, synovitis and arthritis
- Fever
- Increased ESR/ CRP
- MEFV gene mutation for a protein called Pyrin
- Treatment is Colchicine
- Renal amyloidosis with increased risk of renal failure, proteinuria and nephrotic syndrome
- Turkish, Sephardic Jews, Armenians and Arabs

29. Ahi tuna binge with red rash, hot flashes, hives, facial flushing, paresthesia, nausea, vomiting, abdominal pain is scombroid fish poisoning due to histamine in the fish
- Treat with antihistamines
- Due to improperly stored fish such as tuna, mackerel, mahi-mahi, sardines, herring etc.

- Resolves in 1 day

30. Ciguatera fish poisoning is due to a marine algae toxin in fish such as barracuda unlike scombroid fish poisoning has no cure and has prolonged course. It causes nausea, vomiting and tingling in fingers and toes

31. Conscious sedation
    - Medication with the longest duration of action: Demerol/ Meperidine - 3 hours
    - Midazolam 1.5 hours
    - Fentanyl 1 hour
    - Propofol 4-8 minutes

32. Cyclic vomiting syndrome (CVS)
    - History of migraine headaches
    - Lasts 3-6 days and occurs 3-4 times per year
    - Different from Cannabis Hyperemesis syndrome (CHS) in that CHS has no extended periods of well-being
    - Treatment of CVS
        - Abortive: Zofran, Promethazine, Prochlorperazine, Triptans
        - Prophylactics: Tricyclics, Cyproheptadine, Propranolol, Erythromycin and Phenobarbital

33. Palatal torus is a benign condition and no f/u needed

34. Sclerosing mesenteritis
    - Male
    - 5-7th decade of life
    - Palpable abdominal mass, partial small bowel obstruction
    - Most cases relatively benign
    - History of abdominal trauma, surgery, autoimmune disease or abdominal malignancy
    - Imaging studies show mesenteric swirling, misty mesentery
    - Treatment is corticosteroids + Colchicine/ Azathioprine/ Tamoxifen

35. PPI with SVT, seizures and tetany indicates magnesium deficiency
    - Early B12 deficiency has increased homocysteine and increased MMA

36. Zn is present in alkaline phosphatase enzyme

37. Zn deficiency causes acrodermatitis enteropathica which is an inherited skin disease
    - Rash on fingers and toes, perioral, periorbital, perianal and

intertriginous
- Associated with loss of taste (*dysgeusia*)
- Growth retardation, poor wound healing
- Hypogonadism
- Skin, nail and hair changes

38. Vitamin A excess can cause hypertriglyceridemia

39. Celiac artery compression syndrome
    - Dunbar syndrome
    - Median arcuate ligament syndrome
    - Bruit during expiration
    - Thin female 30-50 years of age with pain
    - Angiography is the test of choice with stenosis and post stenotic dilation. May show a hooked celiac artery

40. Chromogranin a
    - Family of acidic proteins which are a major component of secretory granules endocrine and neuroendocrine cells
    - Nonspecific. Chromogranin a is higher in metastatic disease compared to local disease. It may also indicate relapse of the disease.
    - Commonest cause of false positive results are PPI, atrophic gastritis, impaired kidney function, heart diseases, hypertension and rheumatoid arthritis
    - Stop PPIs at least a week before and histamine type 2 receptor antagonist 24 hours before

41. Manganese toxicity with TPN
    - Extrapyramidal symptoms and Parkinson's disease due to involvement of basal ganglia
    - Cholestasis

42. Abdominal bruit, weight loss and symptoms that does not vary with respiration likely has SMA syndrome
    - Symptoms improve with knee chest position, prone or left side
    - Treatment is nutritional support or surgery

43. Commonest source of hemodynamically significant bleed in elderly is Diverticular bleed
    - Treatment is endoscopic clip rather than cautery

44. Flank ecchymosis or Gray-Turner sign with hematoma on the flanks and thighs is suggestive of retroperitoneal bleed

- Check CT scan for retroperitoneal bleed

45. Urticaria pigmentosa is a sign of systemic mastocytosis
    - Check serum histamine
    - Darier's sign
    - Urticaria pigmentosa
    - Enlarged liver due to infiltration
    - Bone marrow biopsies show mast cells which are positive for c-KIT and CD 117

46. Mast cell activation disorder shows increased tryptase in response to
    - Sulfite preservatives in hotdog
    - Dairy
    - Alcohol

47. Metoclopramide
    - Dopamine 2 antagonist like Domperidone which is also a 5HT4 + 5HT3 antagonist
    - Prolongs QT interval
    - 1% Tardive dyskinesia
    - FDA approval for use for 12 weeks
    - Can cause hyperprolactinemia

48. COVID 19
    - Diarrhea in 8% in China, 20% in other countries
    - N/V in 8%
    - No increased risk for IBD population
    - Stool infectivity not confirmed
    - No stool testing recommended
    - Routine SARS-CoV-2 testing prior to endoscopy is no longer needed to perform endoscopy safely

49. COVID mild elevation of transaminases < 5 x normal
    Can also cause a severe form of liver injury via cholangiopathy

50. Standard scope: Chromoendoscopy > white light
    - High-definition scopes: Chromoendoscopy is equal to White light endoscopy

51. Drugs used for management of Alcohol abuse
    - Baclofen
    - Antabuse
    - Naltrexone

52. Planned weight loss in IBS-D
   - Manage by Phentermine and Topiramate
   - Orlistat causes diarrhea, so not appropriate
   - Liraglutide is an injectable drug

53. Gum issues with lower leg rash is Scurvy
   - Acute gastritis with skin lesions and bleeding gums is scurvy

54. Patient on a restrictive diet develops CHF has selenium deficiency

55. Heat stroke can cause abnormal liver enzymes

56. Air in portal vein is ischemic gut

57. Severe CHF, End stage renal disease not on dialysis is ASA 4

58. After 6 weeks of TPN all have sludge and stones
   - Mild elevation in transaminases in 1-2 months
   - Mild increase in ALP after 2-3 weeks
   - Liver failure with TPN after 6 months of TPN therapy

59. TPN with neurological symptoms, consider thiamine deficiency

60. Vitamin A causes hypertriglyceridemia

61. Category D drugs in pregnancy are midazolam/ benzodiazepines

62. Eosinophilic gastroenteritis may be associated with ascites

63. Hyperemesis gravidorum are at a risk of Thiamine deficiency and
Wernicke's encephalopathy
   - Presents with ataxia, oculomotor dysfunction and altered mental status
   - Replace thiamine

64. Niacin deficiency causes Dermatitis, Diarrhea and Dementia (3 D's)
   - Dermatitis with scaly skins over the sun exposed areas of the body is
   known as Pellagra
   - Carcinoid syndrome may cause niacin deficiency

65. In Iron deficiency anemia and negative bidirectional endoscopy, consider
a trial of initial iron supplementation over the routine use of video capsule
endoscopy. (AGA 2020)

- In patients with anticoagulation and/or antiplatelet therapy video capsule endoscopy may be needed to complete work up

66. Thiamine deficiency causes lactic acidosis along with other features such as mental status change or cardiac failure

67. Long history of Crohn's with macrocytic anemia likely has B12 and folate deficiencies
   - Folate and Fe are absorbed in the duodenum

68. Patients on TPN or bypass surgery with hypochromic microcystic anemia and hyperesthesia and weakness of arms and legs likely have Copper deficiency
   - Absorbed in proximal small bowel

69. PPI for GERD may cause magnesium deficiency manifested by carpopedal spasm, seizures and SVT

70. Treat splenic artery aneurysm if
   - Larger than 2 cm
   - Symptomatic
   - During pregnancy

71. Polyarteritis nodosa with ischemic symptoms consider mesenteric angiography
   - Associated with HBV

72. KTW (Klippel-Trenaunay-Weber) syndrome triad
   - Limb hypertrophy
   - Cutaneous hemangioma
   - Varicosities; varicosities of rectum causing life threatening GI bleed
   - Anemia
   - Portal vein hypoplasia

73. HSV of esophagus
   - Intranuclear eosinophilic Cowdry bodies
   - Nuclear molding
   - Nuclear chromatin margination
   - Multinucleated giant cells

74. Eosinophilic gastroenteritis causes ascites, treated by corticosteroids

75. Amyloidosis:
   - Affects duodenum second part in 100%
   - Colorectal and stomach 90%
   - Esophagus 70%
   - Liver in 90% of AL amyloid and 60% of AA amyloid

76. In patients with anemia, use a cutoff of 45 ng/mL over 15 ng/mL when using ferritin to diagnose iron deficiency.
   - In patients with inflammatory conditions or chronic kidney disease, other laboratory tests such as C-reactive protein, transferrin saturation, or soluble transferrin saturation, may be needed in conjunction with ferritin to diagnose iron deficiency anemia. (AGA 2020)

77. In asymptomatic postmenopausal women and men with iron deficiency anemia, recommend bidirectional endoscopy over no endoscopy. (AGA 2020)

78. In asymptomatic premenopausal women with iron deficiency anemia, consider bidirectional endoscopy over iron replacement therapy only. (AGA 2020)
   - Young patients who have other reasons for IDA, iron replacement therapy and no initial bidirectional endoscopy.

79. In iron deficiency anemia without other identifiable etiology after bidirectional endoscopy, noninvasive testing for Helicobacter pylori, followed by treatment if positive, over no testing. (AGA 2020)

80. Patients with iron-deficiency anemia, no routine gastric biopsies to diagnose atrophic gastritis. (AGA 2020)

81. SGLT-2 Inhibitors used for treating DM2 are held for 3 (or 4 for ertugliflozin) days prior to procedures or interventions requiring NPO (fasting) to reduce risk of diabetic ketoacidosis

82. In asymptomatic iron deficiency anemia and plausible celiac disease, serologic testing over routine small bowel biopsies

83. Genes and associations
   - Smad4 associated with juvenile polyp
   - CDH1- Hereditary diffuse gastric ca and lobular breast cancer
   - Chek2 associated with breast and colon cancer
   - ATM, Lynch, STK11, PALB2, BRCA2 associated with Panc Ca

84. Intestinal pseudoobstrution from paraneoplastic syndrome

- Anti-hu or anti-neuronal nuclear ab 1
- Caused by small cell lung ca, carcinoid, lymphoma, renal and ovarian cancers

85. Ileal brake refers to fat in the ileum delays gastric emptying into the small bowel

86. Graft vs host disease on histology
    - Apoptosis, loss of crypts and crypt necrosis
    - Endoscopically edema, erythema, aphthous erosions
    - Diagnosis via flex sig and rectum biopsies

87. Elderly male with elevated ALP but normal GGT. Bone scan to r/o Paget's disease

Procedure related

1. Procedures that carry a high risk of perforation
   - ANY dilation
   - Foreign body removal
   - POEM
   - EMR and ESD
   - Thermal coagulation for hemostasis or tumor ablation
   - Stricture incision
   - ERCP in altered surgical anatomy
   - Self-expanding metal stents
   - Cystgastrostomy or enterostomy using lumen apposing metal stent

2. Perforation closure (AGA 2021)
   - Any unstable patient, delayed perforation or with evidence of peritonitis managed surgically

3. Perforation closure in Esophagus
   - Through the scope clips or over the scope clips for perforations < 20 mm
   - Endoscopic suturing for perforations > 20 mm
   - Esophageal stenting when primary closure is not possible

4. Perforation closure in Stomach
   - Through the scope clips or over the scope clips for perforations <20 mm
   - Endoscopic suturing or clips and endoloops for tears > 20 mm

5. Perforation closure in Duodenum
   - Large type 1 Duodenal tears > 30 mm, surgery consult
   - Type 2 periampullary tears - through the scope clips or coated metal stent in the bile duct across the ampulla

6. Perforation closure in Colon
   - Sigmoid colon tear closed by through or over the scope clips
   - Commonest site of perforation during colonoscopy is sigmoid colon

7. Risk of cardiopulmonary side effects with EGD (ASGE 2022)
   - Age 65 years
   - Obesity
   - Hypertension
   - Diabetes
   - Coronary artery disease in particular, EGD performed within 30 days of an MI
   - Higher ASA scores
   - Monitored anesthesia care

- NO increased risk with obstructive sleep apnea

8. EGD with Food bolus impaction
    - Increased risk of bleeding with use of through the scope instruments vs Push technique (? selection bias)
    - Increased perforation with
        - Longer duration between presentation and EGD
            - Safe usually if EGD is within 24 hours of presentation
        - Food bolus > 3 cm
        - Presence of ingested bone
        - Through the scope instrument to extract bolus (? Selection bias)
        - Use of overtube

9. Risk of perforation in EGD with dilation
    - Male
    - >70 years
    - Malignant strictures
    - Pneumatic dilation for achalasia
    - History of H&N cancer
    - Corrosive injury associated stricture

10. Risk of bleeding with PEG placement (0.6-2.6%)
    - Obesity
    - DM2
    - DAPT or full anticoagulation
        - PEG placement in patient on DAPT is a high risk bleeding procedure
        - Do not stop aspirin but stop Plavix

11. Placement of a larger caliber PEG will NOT solve peristomal leakage

12. Risk of Cellulitis with PEG placement (1.7-3.4%) is mainly with Obesity
    - PEG needs Antibiotic prophylaxis
    - External bolster should free float 1-2 cm from the abdominal wall
    - Gauze placed over and not under the external bolster

13. Inadvertant removal of PEG tube
    - Tract takes at least 4 weeks to mature
        - NO blind replacement of PEG within 4 weeks
    - Replacing a PEG tube may cause diarrhea with refeeding if the tract goes accidentally through the colon and causes colocutaneous fistula
        - Prevented by using both transillumination and finger palpation techniques for placement of PEG initially

14. Buried bumper syndrome
    - Inability to rotate or advance the tube

- Difficulty in feeding through PEG tube and increased leakage around PEG tube
- Due to tight positioning of the external bumper of PEG tube
- The internal bumper is now enveloped by the GI tract
- Schedule endoscopy for PEG tube replacement

15. Percutaneous radiology guided gastrostomy placement has higher risk of
    - 30 day mortality
    - Colonic perforation
    - Bleeding
    - Peritonitis

16. Pneumoperitoneum following PEG placement without peritonitis should not preclude initiation of tube feeds

17. Risk factors for capsule retention (ACG 022)
    - Crohn's disease
    - History of small-bowel obstruction or previous resection
    - Previous abdominal or pelvic radiotherapy
    - Chronic use of a high-dose NSAID
    - Known stricture or mass

18. Indications for capsule endoscopy
    - Overt and occult suspected small-bowel bleeding
    - Iron-deficiency anemia
    - Crohn's disease
    - Refractory celiac disease
    - Surveillance of polyposis syndromes
    - Suspected small-bowel tumors
    - Abnormal small-bowel imaging when DE is contraindicated

19. Low-yield indications for capsule study include
    - Evaluation of abdominal pain
    - Iron-deficiency anemia in the absence of suspected GI bleeding
    - Diarrhea
    - Malabsorption in the absence of known diagnosis

20. Risk of perforation with EUS
    - Trainee involvement
    Operator inexperience
    -Older patient
    - History of difficult esophageal intubation
    - Presence of esophageal malignancy
    - Cervical spine osteophytes

21. Risk of hemorrhage with EUS
   - Antiplatelets
   - Anticoagulants
   - Low-molecularweight heparins
   - Lower GI FNA/ fine-needle biopsy sampling
   - Fiducial placement

22. Risk of infection with EUS with sampling of pancreatic cyst or mediastinum

23. Pancreatitis with EUS in fiducial placement

24. Risk of perforation with lumen apposing metal stent placement in pancreatic fluid collections increases with subsequent necrosectomy (ASGE 2022)

25. For non-lipomatous lesion, EUS is preferred over endoscopy or other modalities
   - EUS with tissue acquisition preferred (FNB or FNA with on site evaluation
   - If EUS is negative then unroofing technique if definitive diagnosis is needed

26. No preference of forward viewing endoscope over oblique viewing scope (Echoendoscopes) for initial evaluation of subepithelial lesion (SEL)
   - Bite on bite biopsies not recommended for SEL

27. For resection of SEL arising from muscularis propria consider submucosal tunneling technique or surgery
   - For GIST < 2 cm endoscopic approach can be considered

28. If a SEL is causing symptoms then resection/ surgery even without pre-resection diagnosis
   - Exception is a large GIST which may benefit from Imatinib

29. Surveillance plan needed for SEL without tissue diagnosis or resection unless there is a high degree of confidence that there is no malignant potential

30. There is no need to stop breastfeeding after Propofol sedation
   - Avoid Demerol during breastfeeding

31. Left ventricular assist device associated with intestinal angiodysplasia

32. Bile acid binding resin used in Post cholecystectomy diarrhea

Obesity management

1. Obesity
   - Class 1 BMI is 30-<35: Intragastric balloons
   - Class 2 BMI is 35-<40
   - Class 3 BMI > 40
   - Gastric aspiration for class 2 or 3
   - Gastric bypass considered for class 2 with comorbidity or class 3

2. Obese patients seeking a weight-loss intervention who have failed a trial of conventional weight-loss strategies, use Intragastric balloon (IGB) therapy with lifestyle modification over lifestyle modification alone. (AGA 2021)
   - Daily 1–2 adult dose multivitamins after IGB placement (AGA 2021)

3. While undergoing IGB therapy, patients need moderate- to high-intensity concomitant lifestyle modification interventions to maintain and augment weight loss (AGA 2021)

4. Prophylaxis with PPI in patients undergoing IGB therapy

5. During IGB therapy, use the intraoperative anesthetic regimens associated with the lowest incidence of nausea along with perioperative antiemetics. Patients also need scheduled antiemetic regimen for 2 week after IGB placement

6. Perioperative laboratory screening for nutritional deficiencies in patients undergoing IGB therapy

7. Contraindications to IGB include previous gastrointestinal surgery, anticoagulation, gastric ulcerations, large hiatal hernias and pregnancy

8. After IGB removal, patients may need subsequent weight-loss or maintenance interventions that include dietary interventions, pharmacotherapy, repeat IGB, or bariatric surgery

9. Obesity with inadequate response to lifestyle interventions, use pharmacological agents with lifestyle interventions rather than continuing lifestyle interventions alone (AGA 2022)
   - Semaglutide 2.4 mg
   - Liraglutide 3.0 mg
   - Phentermine-topiramate ER
   - Phentermine

- Naltrexone-bupropion ER
- Diethylpropion
- NO Orlistat recommended
- Gelesis100 oral superabsorbent hydrogel only in the context of a clinical trial

10. Interval development of a neofundus following gastric sleeve surgery can lead to weight gain

11. After bariatric surgery
   - Increased GLP1 secreted from L cells in dital small bowel and colon that stimulates insulin secretion, inhibits glucagon
   - Increased CCK produced by intestinal I cells, satiety hormone that reduces gastric motility
   - Increased peptide YY (PYY)- increased satiety and decreases appetite

Images and Slides

Please be familiar with images of the following-

1. Image of HRM
   - DL < 4.5 seconds indicates distal esophageal spasm
   - Normal IRP rules out achalasia

2. Slide of collagenous sprue with a collagen band, treated with corticosteroids

3. Jackhammer esophagus- High amplitude with DCI> 8000mm (> 20% of contractions), IRP < 15mm, DL> 4.5s

4. Abetalipoproteinemia has vacuolated villi

5. Image of esophagus with HSV- HSV infection shows multinucleation, nuclear margination and molding

6. Syphilis slide- Dense plasma cell infiltration and mononuclear vasculitis are associated with syphilis. Diagnosed by Warthin-Starry silver stain

7. H pylori- Marked lymphoplasmacytic inflammation and neutrophils associated with chronic active gastritis associated with H pylori

8. CMV associated with cytomegaly and owl's eye intranuclear inclusions

9. Image with candida hyphae

10. Image of Zenker's diverticulum

11. Endoscopic image of EoE

12. Gas in the portal vein consistent with ischemic bowel

13. Barium UGI series of a Duodenal ulcer

14. Fish eye of IPMN and it is equal in incidence in males and females

15. Pancreatogram with skinny beaded pancreatic duct is Autoimmune pancreatitis

16. Ground glass appearance of hepatocytes is HBV managed by entecavir

17. Dark liver on MRI is HH

18. Liver slide with Prussian blue stain for Fe but not in hepatocytes but in sinusoidal Kupffer cells- Transfusion overload

19. Prussian blue stain in Hereditary hemochromatosis (HH) with increased iron in hepatocytes in C282y/c282Y mutation

20. Large cavernous blood-filled spaces in liver is Peliosis hepatis associated with OCP's

21. Liver biopsy slide showing granuloma in liver is sarcoidosis

22. Liver biopsy with onion skinning is PSC
   - Diagnosis is through MRCP

23. CT with a central scar in the liver is FNH

24. Dark pigmented bile casts- anabolic steroids from cholestasis

25. Autosomal recessive disorders with copper stains is Wilson's disease. Neurological symptoms 95% have KF rings

26. Liver cells with microvesicular fat within
   - AFLP
   - Reye's syndrome
   - HAART antiretroviral therapy
   - Tetracycline and massive aspirin use

27. Exuberant inflammation around the bile duct, AMA + is PBC
   - Majority are females

28. Spoke wheel plasma cells- AIH treat with prednisone

29. PAS + stain with reddish globules in hepatocytes
   - A1AT deficiency ZZ phenotype
   - Most with the phenotype never develop disease

30. Steatohepatitis with Mallory bodies
   - Alcohol
   - Metabolic syndrome
   - Tamoxifen
   - Amiodarone
   - Jejunoileal bypass

31. Centrilobular necrosis in INH toxicity

32. Treatment of thrombosed external hemorrhoids is thrombectomy and removal of overlying of skin within 3-4 days of symptoms
   - Grade 3 hemorrhoids treated by band ligation

- Grade 4 non reducible hemorrhoids surgical hemorrhoidectomy

33. Dilated hepatic veins like a maple leaf is right heart failure

34. Image of Mirizzi's syndrome with increased LFTs

35. Porphyria cutanea tarda (PCT)
    - HCV in 90%
    - HCV also associated with Non-Hodgkin's and autoimmune Idiopathic Thrombocytopenic Purpura

36. Sinusoidal dilatation on liver biopsy consistent with OCP and Budd-Chiari syndrome (BCS)

37. Image of pyoderma gangrenosum
    - 20-50% of IBD
    - Independent of disease activity
    - Treatment is local steroids, infliximab, dapsone, tacrolimus and cyclosporine

38. UC patient with a large transverse colon on KUB is toxic megacolon
    - Mortality with perforation is > 40%
    - Mortality without perforation is 10%
    - Treatment is total colectomy

39. Palmar-plantar pustulosis in patient on Anti-TNF and Azathioprine, switch the regimen to Ustekinumab

40. Slide with microabscesses is suggestive of UC.
    - IBD shows branching crypts
    - Treat with mesalamine

41. X-ray of bamboo spine consistent with ankylosing spondylitis is suggestive of IBD

42. Slide with large gastric vacuoles indicating foveolar hyperplasia and large cystic dilatation is Menetrier's disease
    - Hypoalbuminemia
    - Protein losing enteropathy
    - Best test is fecal alpha 1 antitrypsin clearance
    - Hypochlorhydria

43. Barium x-ray with thick gastric folds has gastrinoma

44. GIST tumor on EUS arises from the 4th (hypoechoic - dark) layer of the gut
Duplication cysts are anechoic and arise from 3rd submucosal layer

45. Middle aged person with obscure GI bleed with ileal neoplasm with slides showing solid blue cells, diagnosis is carcinoid and check for chromogranin A

46. Carcinoid of stomach
    - Slide of blue cords of cells
    - Stains for chromogranin A and synaptophysin
    - Type 1 is associated with atrophic gastritis
    - Type 2 is associated with MEN1
    - Type 3 is sporadic which is the most dangerous

47. Endoscopic image of Esophageal acanthosis which is associated with Cowden's syndrome

9. ABBREVIATIONS

ACLF	Acute on Chronic Liver Failure
ADR	Adenoma detection rate
AFAP	Attenuated FAP
AFLP	Acute fatty liver of pregnancy
AFP	Alpha fetoprotein
AIH	Autoimmune hepatitis
ALF	Acute liver failure
ALP	Alkaline phosphatase
AMA	Antimitochondrial antibody
ANA	Antinuclear antibody
APC	Argon plasma coagulation
ARM	Anorectal manometry
ASMA	Anti-smooth muscle antibody
AVM	Arteriovenous malformation
BCS	Budd Chiari syndrome
BE	Barrett's epithelium
BET	Balloon expulsion test
CD	Crohn's Disease
CDI	C diff infection
CEIM	Complete eradication of intestinal metaplasia
CHS	Cannabis hyperemesis syndrome
CKD	Chronic kidney disease
CMV	Cytomegalovirus
CRC	Colorectal cancer
CVA	Cerebrovascular accident
CVS	Cyclic vomiting syndrome
DAPT	Dual antiplatelet therapy
DCI	Distal contractile integral
DD	Defecatory disorder
DES	Distal esophageal spasm
DILI	Drug induced liver injury
DL	Distal latency
DM	Diabetes mellitus
EET	Endoscopic eradiation therapy
EGD	Esophagogastroduodenoscopy
EGJOO	Esophagogastric Junction outlet obstruction
EMR	Endoscopic mucosal resection
EoE	Eosinophilic esophagitis
ES	External anal sphincters
EUS	Endoscopic ultrasound
FAP	Familial adenomatous polyposis
FAP	Familial adenomatous polyposis
FLIP	Functional lumen imaging planimetry
FMT	Fecal microbiota transplant
FNH	Focal nodular hyperplasia
GAVE	Gastric antral vascular ectasia
GB	Gallbladder
GE	Gastroesophageal
GERD	Gastroesophageal reflux disease
GI	Gastrointestinal
GIM	Gastric intestinal metaplasia
GIST	Gastrointestinal stromal tumor
GOO	Gastric outlet obstruction
GP	Gastroparesis

GVHD	Graft versus host disease
H2RA	Histamine2 receptor antagonists
HAV	Hepatitis A virus
HBV	Hepatitis B virus
HCC	Hepatocellular cancer
HCV	Hepatitis C virus
HDS	Herbal and dietary supplements
HELLP	Hemolysis elevated liver enzymes low platelets
HGD	High grade dysplasia
HH	Hereditary Hemochromatosis
HHT	Hereditary hemorrhagic telangiectasia
HNPCC	Hereditary nonpolyposis colon cancer
HRM	High resolution manometry
HRS	Hepatorenal syndrome
HSV	Herpes simplex virus
IBD	Inflammatory bowel disease
ICI	Immune checkpoint inhibitors
IPAA	Ileoanal pouch anastomosis
IRA	Ileorectal anastomosis
IRP	Integrated relaxation pressure
IS	Internal anal sphincters
I-SEE	Index of severity for EoE
LGD	Low grade dysplasia
LMWH	Low molecular weight heparin
LN	Lymph node
LPR	Laryngopharyngeal reflux
LS	Liver stiffness
LT	Liver transplantation
MALTOMA	Marginal B cell Lymphoma
MAP	MUTYH associated polyposis
MEN	Multiple endocrine neoplasia
MMA	Methyl malonic acid
MMC	Migratory motor complex
MSA	Magnetic sphincter augmentation
MSI	Microsatellite instability
MWT	Mallory-Weiss tear
NAC	n-Acetyl cysteine
NAFLD	Nonalcoholic fatty liver disease
NAPQI	n acetyl p benzoquinone imine
NASH	Non-alcoholic steatohepatitis
NERD	Non-erosive reflux disease
NET	Neuroendocrine tumor
NTC	Normal transit constipation
PBC	Primary biliary cholangitis
PJS	Peutz-Jeghers Syndrome
POEM	Peroral endoscopic myotomy
PPI	Proton pump inhibitors
PUD	Peptic ulcer disease
RCT	Randomized Controlled Trial
RRT	Renal replacement therapy
RYGB	Roux-en-Y gastric bypass
SAAG	Serum ascites albumin gradient
SCADD	Segmental colitis associated with diverticular disease
SEL	Subepithelial lesion

SIBO	Small intestinal bacterial overgrowth
SMA	Superior mesenteric artery
SNS	Sacral nerve stimulation
SSP	Sessile serrated polyps
SSRI	Selective serotonin reuptake inhibitors
STC	Slow transit constipation
SVC	Superior vena cava
TBE	Timed barium esophagram
TI	Terminal ileum
TIF	Transoral incisionless fundoplication
TIPS	Transjugular intrahepatic portosystemic shunt
TLESR	Transient lower esophageal sphincter relaxation
TTG	Tissue transglutaminase
TV	Tubulovillous
UC	Ulcerative colitis
UES	Upper esophageal sphincter
UGI	Upper gastrointestinal

If there are any errors or suggestions, please e-mail me at Samslastminuteguide@gmail.com.

Made in United States
Troutdale, OR
11/19/2023

14740142R00146